KU-012-920

Getting the Buggers to Behave

Also by Sue Cowley

How to Survive your First Year in Teaching, second edition
Getting the Buggers into Drama
Getting the Buggers to Think, second edition
Getting the Buggers to Write 2, second edition
Guerilla Guide to Teaching, second edition
Sue Cowley's A–Z of Teaching
Sue Cowley's Teaching Clinic
Letting the Buggers be Creative
Getting your Little Darlings to Behave

Getting the Buggers to Behave

Fourth Edition

SUE COWLEY

SWINDON COLLEGE

LEARNING RESOURCE CENTI

continuum

SWINDON COLLEGE

14th November 2011

LEARNING RESOURCE CENTRE

54050000377499

A companion website to accompany this book is available online at: http://education.cowley.continuumbooks.com

Please visit the link and register with us to receive your password and to access these downloadable resources.

If you experience any problems accessing the resources, please contact Continuum at: info@continuumbooks.com

Continuum International Publishing Group

The Tower Building   80 Maiden Lane
11 York Road   Suite 704
London SE1 7NX   New York NY 10038

www.continuumbooks.com

First edition published 2001, London, UK
Second edition published 2002, London, UK
Third edition published 2006, London, UK
This fourth edition published 2010, London, UK

© Sue Cowley 2010

All rights reserved. No part of this publication may be reproduced or transmitted in any form or by any means, electronic or mechanical, including photocopying, recording, or any information storage or retrieval system, without prior permission in writing from the publishers.

Sue Cowley has asserted her right under the Copyright, Designs and Patents Act, 1988, to be identified as Author of this work.

British Library Cataloguing-in-Publication Data
A catalogue record for this book is available from the British Library.

ISBN: 9781441173140 (paperback)

Library of Congress Cataloging-in-Publication Data
Cowley, Sue.
Getting the buggers to behave / Sue Cowley.—4th ed.
  p. cm.
Includes index.
  ISBN 978-1-4411-7314-0 (pbk.) 1. Classroom management. 2. Behavior modification. I. Title.
  LB3013.C69 2010
  371.102′4—dc22

Typeset by Pindar NZ, Auckland, NZ
Printed and bound in Great Britain by MPG Books Group Ltd

Contents

Part Two: The Teacher and the Teaching

Part Three: The Students and the Setting

Part Four: *When Things get Tough*

Acknowledgements

Many thanks go to all the teachers, staff, children and young people who I've worked with over the years. Your inspiration, ideas, advice and support are the framework on which this book was written. Teaching often seems to run in the family, so I must also thank my marvellous mum and my amazing aunt for inspiring me to go into the profession.

Huge thanks to Alexandra Webster for her support over the years, and to all the team at Continuum, including Melanie Wilson, Anna Fleming, Charlotte Hoare, Liz White and Christina Parkinson. And of course, very special thanks and love to Tilak, Álvie and Edite.

Author's note, fourth edition

It's been over a decade now since I sat down in a small back bed-room in Somerset and wrote this book. I can remember vividly how the words literally spilled out of me and onto the page. In a sense, it was a book that wrote itself: a distillation of all that I'd learnt and experienced in the first part of my teaching career. At that point I'd got through the newly qualified bit, taught overseas, taken on a promoted post, worked in schools where handling behaviour was (in that classic euphemism) a 'challenge'. I'd found what I thought were some useful strategies for dealing with behav-iour, and I wanted to share them with the world.

In the time that's gone by since then, I've been fortunate enough to work with literally thousands of people in the world of education. Not just newly qualified and experienced teachers, but also teaching assistants, support staff, early years practitioners, librarians, further education tutors, university lecturers, senior managers, trainee teachers, and many others who help children, young people and adults to learn. I've also had a couple of kids of my own, so I've seen the world of education through the eyes of a parent as well.

Through all these experiences, I've picked up loads more great ideas about how to manage behaviour. I've also gained an insight into what works in different settings, with different young people, and for different kinds of staff. The basic tenets of this book remain faithful to the original. What I've done is adapt and develop the ideas so that they apply to more practitioners, in more diverse situations: to those working in early years and further education, as well as primary and secondary schools. And for those of you working in the most challenging schools or colleges, I've included a new section on coping in really difficult circumstances. I've also taken advantage of new developments in the world of technology. So, there's also a companion website for this book, offering you extra material, links and ideas.

At its heart, though, this is still a book of *practical* ideas, of *realistic* strategies that you can put to immediate use in your work. Still no theory – I promise – and only passing reference to the latest forms and fads and acronyms from the world of behaviour management (these move so quickly that they would be out of date between writing this book and it being published). You might not agree with everything I say here (please don't), but grab what suits, give it a go, and I sincerely hope it helps you in getting your children/pupils/students/young people/learners/buggers – whatever you wish to call them! – to behave.

Sue Cowley
www.suecowley.co.uk

Introduction

With a well-behaved class, teaching is one of the most wonderful jobs in the world. Every day offers you a new and different experience: the chance to see your students discover fresh concepts, to learn something they never knew before, the opportunity to make a real difference to their lives. Unfortunately, with a badly behaved class, it becomes much harder to enjoy your job. You're in the classroom to teach, but unless you can get behaviour sorted first, you can't fulfill that role. One of the most essential characteristics of a good, effective teacher is the ability to manage the behaviour of a class, so that the students can get on with learning. This book can help by offering you a wealth of practical ideas to do just that, to try out in your own classroom.

Teachers use a wide range of skills in their everyday work: you need to be a specialist at teaching your subjects, you must be a skilled communicator, and you need to manage the behaviour of your class. At its heart, behaviour management is about relationships – building them, sustaining them, working on them, even when you meet a student who has no interest in relating to you in return. To an extent, you learn to do it through being in the classroom. As time goes on, and you gain in experience, you find yourself drawing from a bank of ideas and strategies to help you. There are some teachers who are naturally good at regulating behaviour, who have an innate ability to engage with and 'hold' a class. But it's also possible to improve and increase your behaviour management skills, whatever your starting point, and that is exactly what this book will help you do.

This book is practical, down-to-earth and easy to read. No

academic theory – just lots of tips, advice and examples to show how the ideas I give work in practice. Although I address my suggestions mainly to teachers, you might also find this book helpful if you work in any role within education (as a classroom assistant, a school librarian, a lunchtime supervisor, and so on). The ideas and advice given here are based on common-sense observations and strategies that have worked for me. There is no 'magic solution', no 'silver bullet' waiting for you in these pages – just honest and realistic advice. My hope is that you find this book a useful reference guide – one that you can turn to for ideas when you need them, or to find alternative strategies for dealing with your students. There is also material on the companion website, including some ideas about why students misbehave, some feedback from student interviews on which behaviour management strategies they believe work best, and a discussion about how students' behaviour changes as they progress through their schooling.

Teachers today are stressed – by the workload, the paperwork, and, of course, the behaviour. What I give you in this book are some ways of minimizing the stress: that's why this book focuses mainly on strategies for *you*, rather than for your students. What I'm interested in doing is helping you survive day to day in a challenging job, and allowing you to enjoy the amazing career you have chosen. I do hope that this book helps you in getting your students to behave. Because if you can get it at least partly right, not only will you improve the chances for each of your students, but you'll also be able to thrive and flourish in the wonderful career you've chosen.

Please note: to simplify things, in this book I use the word 'student' to apply to whoever it is you're teaching. To you they might be children, pupils, teenagers, young people, learners, adults: 'student' was the most all-encompassing term I could find. Similarly, I use male/female in alternate chapters to refer to the teacher, again to simplify things for the reader.

PART ONE

In the Beginning

1

The basics of behaviour management

What are the basics?

In this first chapter, I take a look at the basics, the fundamental ground rules of behaviour management. These techniques need to become intuitive if you hope to get consistently good behaviour. Indeed, this is why experienced teachers sometimes seem to have a 'magic' touch with their classes. They are doing these things instinctively: the strategies have become a subconscious part of their teaching. That is not to say that doing these things will automatically *guarantee* you good behaviour, but you stand a much better chance of getting it once they are in place.

The basics are:

> Be definite: *'I know what I want.'*
> Be aware: *'I know what will happen if I do/don't get what I want.'*
> Be calm and consistent: *'I'm always polite and fair to you.'*
> Give them structure: *'I know where we're going.'*
> Be positive: *'You're doing great.'*
> Be interested: *'You're people as well as students.'*
> Be flexible: *'I know when to bend rather than break.'*
> Be persistent: *'I refuse to give up.'*
> Engage them: *'I want you to want to learn.'*

If you're new to our noble profession, the basics will give you a great foundation for the journey you're about to take. They're essentially a set of common-sense ideas about managing behaviour, and about building good relationships. All these ideas are developed from my own experiences of teaching children, young people and adults, and from seeing how others do it too. If you've been in education for a while, and you're experiencing problems with behaviour, take a look at the basics to see whether you're overlooking something simple.

Be definite

'I know what I want.'

The first and perhaps the most important of my basics is that you've got to come across to your students as being someone who knows what she wants. There are three parts to this. You've got to:

> 1 Know what you expect from your students.
> 2 Communicate it to them so there are no ambiguities.
> 3 Give them the perception that you are confident about getting what you've asked for.

If you think about it, it's only fair – you can't claim that your students are 'misbehaving' unless you've made it clear what 'behaving' looks like in the first place. Let's take a look at the three aspects in turn:

1. Know what you expect from your students

This is harder than it sounds, especially when you first start out in teaching. You might worry about whether it's fair to ask younger children to sit still on the carpet with arms and legs crossed, or to request that older students work for a while in complete silence. In theory, the behaviour policy at your particular school or setting should outline the rules. Certainly there will be some 'absolutes' – whole-school edicts on mobile phones, chewing gum, swearing, and so on.

But although this gives you a starting point, in reality you have to establish your own set of standards, to work out what your own expectations are. Much will depend on your choice of teaching style (see Chapter 5 on p. 73). If you're working in a tough situation, you'll also have to sort out a list of priorities: what really matters, and what can be left until you've established a relationship with the group? If you're a secondary teacher working with students of different ages, your expectations of your youngest class may be different to your expectations of your oldest. It can take a good couple of years to really get this all worked out in your mind.

It's probably most helpful at this point if I give you my own top three expectations of how a group should behave. These apply equally to when I'm working with children, young people, or adults, although the way that I express them will differ.

✓ *I expect you to listen* – to pay silent attention when anyone is addressing the whole group
✓ *I expect you to be respectful* – to each other, to me, to yourself
✓ *I expect you to give it a go* – to work to the best of your ability

And in return, you must try your very hardest to fulfil these expectations as well.

As well as these general behaviours, it also pays to be really specific about every single thing that students do in your lessons. If you don't give exact details of what you want, they will have to work it out for themselves (probably by messing around until you do specify what you wanted). It is far better to be clear from the word 'go'. Don't introduce too many expectations at the start; instead, you can drip-feed them in as you need. For instance, the first time you do group work, talk about how this should be done; the first time you line up the class, talk about how they should do this, and so on.

2. Communicate it to them so there are no ambiguities
Once you know exactly what you want, you've got to get it across to the class, using clear, simple and meaningful language. A great way to do this is to use 'I expect', 'I want' or 'I need' statements, again depending on the kind of style you wish to communicate.

'I expect' would come across as slightly authoritarian, whereas 'I need' is a bit softer and more of a request than a demand. Alternatively, you might decide to phrase your expectations using 'we' ('we always listen'), to give a sense of the whole group working together. This works particularly well with young children.

Some teachers like to work out their expectations together with the class. So long as this doesn't muddy the waters, or take too much time, it can work really well. Often, though, you are essentially just getting the students to come up with the rules that you wanted yourself in the first place. Sometimes, it is quicker and simpler just to tell them!

3. Give them the perception that you are confident about getting what you've asked for

Like predators sensing a weakness in their prey, students are instinctively aware of uncertainty in their teachers. (Think back to when you were at school – I bet there were some teachers you knew you could push around, and others you knew you couldn't.) A key part of achieving your expectations is to communicate an air of confidence to your class. Some people are able to do this naturally; others find it a real struggle and it takes them a few years to get this sorted. It has a lot to do with how well you use verbal and non-verbal communication. In short, some of the strategies you're after include:

- ✓ Plenty of eye contact
- ✓ A clear and engaging tone of voice
- ✓ Lots of movement around the space
- ✓ Open and relaxed body language
- ✓ A refusal to overreact, or to become defensive.

I come back to all these ideas later on in this book, particularly in Chapters 4 and 5.

Of course, there will be situations where, despite your best efforts, some, many or most of the students refuse to comply with your expectations. At these times it is very tempting to give up, to say 'whatever' and just let the students behave as they wish. But maintaining high standards and refusing to give up on your expectations is, in the long run, the key to success. It tells your students that you believe they are capable of great things, and that you won't allow them to let themselves down.

When you first start out in teaching, you may be inclined to play the role of friend rather than authority figure. You might feel that it is somehow unfair to make demands of your students. But actually, you're doing them a favour by giving them clear boundaries. Young people want certainty from the adults in their lives. They need you to create and enforce boundaries to give them a feeling of security. This is often particularly true for your most difficult students, who probably lack structure in their home lives.

Be aware

'I know what will happen if I do/don't get what I want.'

The second of my basics deals with what happens when your students are, or are not, meeting your expectations. Hopefully, at least some of the time, most of your students will be meeting your expectations. When this happens, don't just breathe a silent sigh of relief and stay quiet in the hope that it continues. Acknowledge their good behaviour – note and reward it to encourage them to behave in this way again. One of the simplest and most valuable rewards of all, where the class respects the teacher, is to give them specific, detailed praise. ('That's brilliant, Year 6, every single one of you is listening really well today. I'm really pleased with all of you.')

Some of the time, however, you will have at least a few students who are *not* doing what you want. The way you react when this happens has a powerful influence on your overall chances of success in managing behaviour. When you face low-level misbehaviour, you have three basic options:

1   **The instinctive reaction**: get cross and turn straight to sanctions – this is the reaction you have to fight. Far better to stay calm and deal with the problem in low-level ways, using (2) or (3) below.
2   **The rational reaction**: look around for what's going right,

highlighting any examples of good behaviour ('That's great, Joe, you're waiting silently for the lesson to begin. You obviously want to go to break on time.')
3 **The creative reaction**: think 'how can I deal with this differently?', and use a non-verbal signal, distraction, etc.

Clearly, there will be occasions when sanctions are necessary – when the misbehaviour justifies an instant response. In these circumstances, you must understand the options available to you. Both you and your students must be certain about this: behaviour 'X' leads to consequence 'Y', every time it happens. You need your students to understand the connection between their current misbehaviour and the sanction they will receive if it continues. This puts the choice in their hands: if they understand the rules and the consequences, it is up to them whether or not to comply.

The sanction you use depends on the policy of the school or setting where you work, and on the age of the student involved, for instance:

✓ Early years: a disappointed look, a short time-out
✓ Primary: a yellow/red-card system, missing free choice or 'golden' time
✓ Secondary: a break-time detention, being put 'on report'
✓ Further education: being given a 'disciplinary' warning.

If a student challenges your expectations, try the following:

✓ Be *definite* about what you want, and stick to it
✓ Remain calm and polite throughout the encounter
✓ Clarify any potential misunderstandings
✓ State what will happen if the student refuses to do as you ask
✓ Don't get distracted from your original point
✓ Don't get drawn into a discussion
✓ Depersonalize things – it's about the behaviour, not the person
✓ Sound sad or disappointed about having to give a sanction
✓ If necessary, apply the sanction
✓ If appropriate, offer a 'way out'.

Here's an example to show what I mean. This is based on a typical lower-secondary-school scenario: a defiant student refusing to do as she's asked. Throughout the book you'll find lots of examples based on other age groups.

Ella arrives at the drama studio and walks in without taking off her shoes. The teacher has set a rule that students take off their shoes before entering.

Teacher:	Ella, please go back outside and take off your shoes. [*She states her expectation clearly.*]
Ella:	I can't, Miss.
Teacher:	Come on, Ella, you know the rule in drama that we take off our shoes. Look, everyone's ready, let's get on with the lesson. [*She restates her expectation, rather than asking why Ella can't take off her shoes.*]
Ella:	But I've sprained my ankle. I can't take them off.
Teacher:	Do you have a note about your ankle? [*She checks the truth of this but refuses to be distracted.*]
Ella:	No.
Teacher:	Then please go back outside and take off your shoes. [*She restates her original request.*]
Ella:	No. I won't. Are you gonna make me?
Teacher:	Oh Ella, if you won't take off your shoes, I'll have to pass a red slip to your head of year. Don't make me do that. [*She refuses to get riled, but has had enough of this.*]
Ella:	That's not fair.
Teacher:	Last chance [*pulls out red slip*], three . . . two . . . one. [*Ella grudgingly takes off her shoes.*]

Just to show how differently this encounter might have turned out, let's rerun the scene . . .

Teacher:	Ella, go back outside and take off your shoes.
Ella:	I can't, Miss.
Teacher:	What do you mean, 'I can't'? Of course you can. [*She asks a pointless rhetorical question.*]

11

Ella:	But I've sprained my ankle, Miss. I really can't take them off.
Teacher:	Don't be so stupid. Just get on with it. [*She's dismissive, rather than checking if this is true.*]
Ella:	Don't call me stupid.
Teacher:	Look, just go outside and take off your shoes. Now! [*She's starting to get really cross.*]
Ella:	No. I won't. You gonna make me?
Teacher:	Right, that's it. Go to the head of year. Get out of my sight! [*Ella stomps off, swearing under her breath.*]

Be calm and consistent

'I'm always polite and fair to you.'

We all welcome calmness and consistency: we like to know what to expect from the people in our lives, and it throws us if we get an unpredictable response. For some poorly behaved children, this is the problem they face at home – they never know what the reaction to their behaviour will be. Our duty as professionals is to provide our students with a calm, consistent and considered role model of adult behaviour and responses.

It's not easy for you to be fair and polite all the time – staying calm in the face of misbehaviour can be very hard. This is because of the fight-or-flight response. The student or class 'attacks' you by messing around. You experience a rush of adrenaline and feel the urge to attack back. Alternatively, you want to run away from the situation. Neither of these options is available to us – we can't lash out, and we can't leave.

Although it's difficult, the hard truth is that, if you can remain tirelessly calm and consistent at all times, there is far less chance of serious confrontations arising. You also avoid creating unnecessary stress for yourself. An excellent rule of thumb is to treat your children as you would treat another adult (for instance if you worked in an office) no matter how poorly they behave towards you.

To help yourself stay calm, devise your own techniques and methods to short-circuit that fight-or-flight response. You could:

✓ Take a few deep breaths
✓ Count to ten
✓ Look out of the window to remind yourself that there is a world beyond this room!

As well as staying calm, you've also got to be consistent, and again this is much harder to do than it might sound. Students are extremely sensitive to the idea of fairness. Some will feel that they are unfairly singled out and that, once they have misbehaved, they get picked on over and over again. If we are honest, it's only natural that we like some students more than we like others. The secret, of course, is to treat all of them equally despite any personal preferences we might feel.

Consistency is a bit of a 'holy grail' for headteachers and senior managers, and with good reason. Where a group of staff apply the rules and consequences in a completely consistent way, the students are presented with a single set of standards. But if behaviour 'X' is okay with one person and not with another, then the students get confused about where the boundaries lie. You can support your fellow staff by being as consistent as you can possibly be.

Give them structure

'I know where we're going.'

Our natural impulse is to place a structure on our lives – a daily pattern that gives us a feeling of safety and security. For the most difficult students in our schools, this structure is probably missing from their worlds. At home, their parents or guardians may not have set boundaries for them, or they may constantly move the goalposts, reacting in a variety of different ways to the same types of misbehaviour. Schools offer these young people a refuge, a place where they meet adults who give them suitable and consistent guidelines about what good behaviour actually is.

There are lots of ways you can offer structure to your students: through clear lesson content, through classroom organization, through the methods used to control behaviour. Once you have a clear structure in your own mind, this clarity will be apparent to your class through your high level of awareness and confidence. In addition, make it clear to your students at every stage exactly how and why structures are being used.

If you can achieve a sense of purpose, clarity and structure, this has a number of ongoing benefits, which build one on another:

Your students know what to expect from time spent with you

They begin to view you as a stable feature of their lives; this leads to increased trust and better relationships

They look forward to spending time with you

They look forward to spending time with you

Their behaviour becomes more predictable

Patterns of good behaviour are repeated and become habits.

Here are some areas of your teaching you can structure, and examples of the routines you might use with different age groups:

✓ **Start of day/lesson**: circle time, register, lining up outside the room, starter activity
✓ **Use of space**: carpet time, groupings, layout of desks, seating plans
✓ **The learning**: use of objectives, success criteria, plenary at the end of lesson time
✓ **The resources**: how these are collected, where they are stored, use of volunteers to hand out as a reward

✓ **Expected learning behaviours**: students working quietly, staying in seats, hands up to give an answer, use of talk partners
✓ **End of sessions**: homework set, students stand behind chairs, leaving one by one, story time, playing a short game.

Be positive

'You're doing great!'

'Stress the positive' is, or should be, a bit of a mantra for teachers. The whole area of rewards is a tricky one, which I deal with in detail in Chapter 6. It can sometimes feel as though we are praising our students for just about anything, to try to get them on our side. But this is a mistake: if we set our sights low, then this low level is where our students will aim. If we have high standards, and expect great things, our students learn to strive for their best. Being positive is not just about praising your students, it's also about having a positive outlook during your time with them. The discriminating use of praise, and the ability to remain relentlessly positive, will help you a great deal in managing behaviour. It should also make you less susceptible to stress and negative emotions in your work.

Here are a few of my top tips for staying positive with your students:

✓ Greet your class with a positive expectation – 'Great to see you, we're going to do some fantastic stuff today!'
✓ Expect the best from your class, rather than anticipating the worst.
✓ Frame what you say in a positive light.
✓ Avoid accusing your students or criticizing them.
✓ Tread very carefully with sarcasm and avoid it completely with younger students.
✓ React to misbehaviour by suggesting a positive alternative.
✓ Use praise of individuals to encourage the whole group.
✓ Use rewards in preference to sanctions as far as possible.
✓ Set targets to give positive ways for students to improve.
✓ See completion of targets as a chance to give a reward.

Here are two examples of the same situation, a teacher inviting a class into the room, to show the difference between a positive and a negative approach.

✗ *Negative*

> *'Come on, hurry up! Why are you being so slow? Come on, come on, we've got loads to get through today and we'll never get everything done if you're this slow. What's wrong with you? Why are you making so much noise?'*

I know how I'd feel about being in this teacher's class – inclined to misbehave! Immediately, the students are criticized for being slow. The teacher then creates a negative feeling about the work they will be doing, by putting the blame on the students for not being able to get through it all. Finally, she uses two negative questions to suggest that the students are always this bad. By starting the lesson in such a negative frame of mind, the teacher's expectations may well be met.

✓ *Positive*

> *'Right, if you can all come in as quickly as possible. I've got some really exciting things for you to do today, and we need to get started straight away, so that we can get through them all. That's an excellent level of noise. Well done. Now let's see if you can be even quieter.'*

Here, the teacher tells the students how she wants them to come into the room. She then creates a sense of purpose and interest, by telling them that she has some 'really exciting' things planned for them. Finally, she praises them for the low level of noise, but sets them the challenge of being even quieter. By starting the lesson in this way, a positive atmosphere will hopefully be created and sustained.

Be interested

> *'You're people as well as students.'*

At its heart, good behaviour management is about good teacher/ student relationships. After all, you hopefully came into teaching at least partly because you love working with children, young people, or just people in general. If your students respect you, and feel that you respect them, this will inevitably lead to better behaviour. A key part of building respect is to take an interest in what makes your students tick – to care about what makes them remarkable as individual people, as well as them just being students passing through your bit of the education system.

Taking an interest in your students is particularly helpful when you are experiencing behaviour problems. If a whole class is messing you around because they find a topic or subject boring, then you might be able to incorporate some elements of their latest interest into the learning. Whether it's superheroes, dinosaurs, Transformers, Facebook, music – whatever 'floats their boat' as the saying goes. If an individual child is giving you grief, take an interest in what motivates that student, this will help you devise a suitable reward system.

To make better connections with your students, try:

✓ Asking them about their interests
✓ Getting involved in extra-curricular activities
✓ Keeping up to date with trends
✓ Being open to their ideas, and interested in their opinions.

Be flexible

'*I know when to bend rather than break.*'

There are times as a teacher when you need to learn how to bend a little, for your students' sake and also for your own. Achieving a balance between this flexibility, and the certainty, clarity and consistency already discussed, is one of the hardest and most subtle of all teaching skills. Sometimes, and only sometimes, you will need to relax your boundaries and accept that you are not going to achieve everything that you had initially hoped. By giving a little leeway when it is appropriate, your students will develop greater respect for you as a person and as a teacher.

A flexible approach means you tend to find more inventive and interesting ways around problems. Rather than coming at an issue head-on, and refusing to budge or adapt, be willing to take a lateral approach if that is going to work better. It's about being flexible in your thinking, and in your teaching, to help you manage behaviour. For instance, say you have a Year 2 class who are always tricky last thing on a Thursday afternoon in the summer term, partly because they get tired, and also because by that stage in the week the room is really hot and stuffy. You might battle on regardless, getting into rows and damaging the good relationship you normally have with them. Alternatively, you might apply a bit of flexibility and take them into the hall or playground for this time, doing practical rather than written work.

Flexibility is very much a matter of personal taste and individual circumstances – about knowing when it is appropriate to compromise. In some situations, students respond very well to a teacher who bends a little on occasions; in some settings, the students see any flexibility as a cue to start pushing at the boundaries. In some very challenging schools, where misbehaviour is a complex and deep-rooted issue, taking a 'zero tolerance' approach would mean being left with only a handful of students to actually teach. Trust your judgement on this – don't see it as a personal failure if you have to bend more than you might wish to stay afloat.

There are various situations in which you might offer flexibility to your students:

✓ *With the class*: if your class is never in the mood for work on Friday afternoons, you will achieve very little if you cannot learn to be flexible. Accept that this situation is outside your control. Aim to achieve a very reasonable amount of work, negotiating targets and talking about how fair you are being. Many primary teachers set this time up as a reward, using a period of 'golden time' last lesson of the week to help them manage behaviour in other lessons.

✓ *With the work*: on occasions, when your class has a good reason not to be in the mood to work, you might like to offer a compromise. If the students can complete a specified part of the activity, you could allow them to chat quietly for a few minutes at the end of the lesson as a reward. With older students, you could frame this time as their 'golden time' (a 'chill out time' if you like). This could be time that they must earn with good behaviour, or that they could lose if they don't get the work done.

✓ *With the individual*: some students simply do not want to be in education: it seems entirely irrelevant to their lives. In these situations, find a balance – set small and achievable targets, but don't beat yourself up if a student decides to completely opt out. Where a very troubled student is always confrontational with you, particularly when you use sanctions, try backing off for a while to give you both a break.

In teaching, there's a tricky balance to be struck between the consistency I described earlier in this chapter, and the flexibility that is so essential for day-to-day survival. A good way to think about it is that you have to differentiate your approaches to behaviour management, just as you would differentiate the activities you set for learning. This doesn't mean adapting or dropping your standards; it means you go about achieving those standards in a variety of ways, depending on the individual needs of the student.

Be persistent

'I refuse to give up.'

The ideas and approaches that I give in this book are not a magic panacea – a formula that guarantees instant success. Whatever the theorists say, there is no such thing when it comes to managing behaviour. Even if you put all the advice in this book into practice, you will still experience some problems with behaviour. It's human nature you're dealing with, after all, in all its majestic complexity.

This is where being persistent comes in:

✓ Don't give up on the strategies because they don't work immediately.
✓ Remember, all the time you are working on your behaviour

management skills, you are becoming a better, more effective teacher.

✓ Every time something goes wrong, see this as a learning opportunity – do things differently next time round.

In some very challenging schools, where getting good behaviour is a constant battle, there will be days when you feel like throwing in the towel. It is very tempting indeed to give up on your key expectations, simply because there is so much disruption going on that you don't know where to begin. But the moment that the students see you think 'talk while I talk, I don't care' or 'it doesn't matter if you're disrespectful', then you are effectively giving up on them, and on yourself.

Sometimes you may come across 'the class from hell': a class which, for some reason, contains a large number of really difficult students, or an awkward mix. Again, it's very hard to keep going, to keep plugging away at behaviour and insisting on certain standards, but you have to try. Similarly, some children will apparently throw all your efforts straight back in your face. Never lose sight of the fact that some students have pretty horrible lives outside of school. Try as hard as you can not to give up on the student who always pushes you away, but accept that you can't change the world for everyone.

Engage them

'I want you to want to learn.'

When things are going well, it's relatively easy to find interesting ideas for activities, and to feel inspired about your planning. It's not so easy when your class is being difficult, or when students are misbehaving. But actually, this is the time when it is most crucial. 'Engaging them' is about finding activities that make your students feel interested, excited, curious, puzzled, amused, or just generally in the frame of mind to learn. This is *not* to say that every lesson you ever teach should be an all-singing, all-dancing festival of fun. Nor am I saying that if your students misbehave it is your fault for not making the lesson engaging enough. But when you do interest and enthuse your students, you are *more likely* to encourage them to behave properly. At the very least, it's got to be worth a try.

To engage your students, you need to:

- ✓ Get creative with what goes on in your lessons.
- ✓ Find ways to make the learning fun.
- ✓ Be brave enough to use original, experimental activities.
- ✓ Use interesting and engaging resources.
- ✓ Think laterally about how to present new concepts and ideas.

Think carefully about what holds you back from being more experimental, and how you might deal with these concerns. Are you worried:

- − About what others will think?
- − About the students getting overexcited?
- − About making too much noise or mess?
- − About the class getting out of control?

Consider ahead of time how you would deal with these issues. Ask yourself too: 'What is the worst that could happen?' Clearly you don't want to put yourself or your students at unnecessary risk, but at the same time you've got to put your trust in them if you want to push forward with learning and behaviour. For lots more on the link between high-quality learning and behaviour, see Chapter 7 on p. 101.

2

Managing the first meeting

Why is the first meeting so important?

Your first meeting with any class offers you the chance to sow the seeds for an easy year, or to take the first step on the road to disaster. Every teacher surely knows that hollow feeling in the pit of the stomach, as you let a new class into your room, aware that what you do in that first meeting will have such a long-term impact. Often, both the teacher and the students are at their most nervous or defensive in the first lesson together. You may be anticipating poor behaviour from a 'difficult' group; they may be expecting you to dislike them if they know that other teachers have found them to be a problem.

In an early years setting, your first meeting is typically with an individual child, rather than with a whole class or group (except for when you start a new job at a new setting). Even so, the connection that you make when you first meet a child and his parents is going to be vital in establishing a positive ongoing relationship. Whatever setting you work in, adapt the advice given in this chapter to suit your needs.

With some classes, the first few meetings offer you a 'honeymoon period', where your students are getting to know you, checking you out before revealing their characters in full. It's good advice not to start out with an overly relaxed attitude (although hard to do when you're new to the profession). If you are too laid-back you may find that, a few lessons into the year, the students start to push at the boundaries.

Sometimes you can find yourself in a situation where the

students misbehave for new teachers, testing them to see whether they can withstand the ordeal. This makes life difficult: it's hard to establish your expectations of behaviour with a class who refuse to listen. If you find yourself in this situation, turn to others to help and support you.

What do you need to know before the first meeting?

Teachers are put in a difficult position at the start of a school year (or at the start of the term, if they begin a new job midway through the year). We are expected to meet, control and teach a group of people about whom we know little or nothing. Because of this, there is often a tendency to learn by our mistakes, dealing with problems as they arise, rather than anticipating and trying to resolve them beforehand.

Time is short at the start of term, with staff busy setting up their rooms, doing planning, emptying in-trays, and so on. However, this first meeting with your new group is so important that it pays to take some time out to prepare. Before you meet a new class, you could find out about:

✓ **Potential behaviour issues**: are there well-known 'characters' in the class? If you know that person's name, and what is likely to set him off, you can keep an eye out for the early signs of boundary testing. Make sure you give everyone the chance of a fresh start, though: judge them solely on how they behave for you. Sometimes, older students claim to be proud of having a reputation. Try turning this situation on its head: 'Jason, great to meet you, I've heard so many good things about you. I'm really looking forward to working with you.'

✓ **Learning needs**: aim to find out whether any students have non-behavioural special educational needs that could have an impact on their learning and potentially on their behaviour. (You should be given a list of those children with special educational needs (SEN), and details of what these needs are. If you are not, approach the member of staff responsible for SEN for this information.) If you're not aware of a specific learning need, you might wrongly perceive it as a behavioural issue. For instance, a student with weak literacy skills may not complete the work set in the time available. This could be interpreted as 'laziness' unless the teacher understands the background situation.

✓ **Physical needs:** know about any students with physical difficulties and take them into consideration. Don't assume that students are always confident enough to tell you about their needs, particularly young children. Physical needs could include students who have hearing difficulties or visual impairment. Adapt seating arrangements for students who need to be close to the front of the room.

✓ **Some names:** it's very useful to know the names of one or two of your students before you meet them. Even better, if you're good at memory tricks, learn the names of the whole class, and claim to be a magician ('Is there a Joe in this class? And a Jack?'). Knowing your students' names is vital for behaviour management: start learning them right away. I've included some ideas for how to learn names on p. 34–6.

While pursuing knowledge is very useful, never prejudge a class. This could put you in a negative frame of mind for the first encounter. It's also unfair on the students. Some students who gain a bad reputation early on never get a chance to prove this reputation false. Tell the class you hope they will impress you and you may be pleasantly surprised.

Establishing your teaching style

The more experienced you become as a teacher, the clearer you get about the teaching style you want to use. A fully developed teaching style is something that comes with time and practice. But before you meet a class for the first time, have at least some idea about the style of teaching you want to offer them. After all, from the first moment they meet you, your children are making decisions about you, based on the signals you send through your teaching style.

You need to adapt the style you use according to your individual work situation. There are many possible variables to consider: the type and ethos of the setting, the students' age, your own personality, and so on. I explore the concept of effective teaching and useful teaching styles in lots of detail in Chapters 4 and 5. In your first meeting, some areas are under immediate examination:

- **How you appear**: are you smart, wearing a suit, or do you dress casually? (Either is fine, it just depends on the appropriate attire for your age group.) Are you ready to meet and teach the class, or flustered and bad tempered when they arrive? Interviewers make snap judgements about candidates in the first few minutes of an interview, based mainly on how they look. If you want your class to behave, you need to make a good impression at this first meeting.
- **The way you talk**: do you sound relaxed or stressed out when you speak? Does your voice sound timid, confident or too loud? Do you use an interesting range of tone and pace to give interest to what you say? Our voices give away a huge amount about our emotional state, especially when we are tense or under pressure.
- **The way you stand and move**: are you relaxed and making good use of the space? Or do you stand frozen at the front, backed up against the wall in a defensive posture? Does your body language signal aggression or self-confidence? Your students will be reading these signals subconsciously to help them decide how to behave for you.
- **The way you treat your students**: do you see your students as equals, or do you have an authoritarian manner? Do you respect people and talk to them politely, maintaining a good example of a role model, whatever the provocation? Do you stay calm when handling any incidents? Remember, when you deal with individual students, the others watch to see how you handle them. Your students are making decisions, based on what they see, about how to behave for you in the future.
- **The way you start and finish sessions**: are you ready and waiting calmly when the group arrives? Or are you unprepared and flustered instead? Do you run out of time at the end of the

lesson and let the class rush out of the room when the bell goes? Or does your session end in a controlled way? Do you put the students in a good mood from the first minute they meet you? And do they leave you feeling that they have had a positive experience, one they want to repeat?

- **The way you teach**: are the activities varied, interesting, challenging and fun? Or do you talk for far too long, so the students get bored and start to mess around? I know you can't make every single lesson totally engaging, but try hard to make at least some of them really great. If you captivate your students early on, they come to your class in a constructive frame of mind, ready and eager to learn.
- **The way you keep control**: with one of you and lots of them, you do need to take control of the situation. But how do you go about doing this? Are you a 'strict and scary' teacher, loud from the first moment you meet the class? Are you firm but fair, controlling them through the strength of your personality? Or perhaps you're 'comic and quirky', the kind of 'character' teacher they're going to have fun with? For much more on these different styles, take a look at Chapter 5.

Establishing your expectations

Having clear expectations, and sharing these with your class, is a key factor in effective behaviour management. In the first few meetings you are defining the boundaries: 'this is acceptable behaviour and this is not'. Or, to put it another way: 'here's a line, just make sure you don't step over it.' By establishing your expectations you show that you are fully in charge of your classroom or teaching space. Your students really do want and appreciate a sense of certainty and clarity from you about what is expected.

An excellent way to explain your expectations is to make statements about what you want. Phrase your statements in the right way for the age group you're working with – use your professional judgement about what will work best. Choose three expectations to have of your students for the first time you meet them, perhaps spend some time talking together about why it's important for them to do these things. Your statements could be:

Early years/lower primary

✓ 'We always listen to each other.'
✓ 'We walk, we don't run.'
✓ 'We are kind to each other and we share.'

Upper primary/lower secondary

✓ 'I expect you to pay complete, silent attention when someone is addressing the whole group.'
✓ 'I expect you to stay in your seats at all times, unless you have my permission to get up.'
✓ 'I expect you to work to the best of your ability.'

Upper secondary/further education

✓ 'I need you all to listen, so we can get on with learning.'
✓ 'I want to see respectful attitudes from everyone.'
✓ 'I need to hear appropriate language at all times.'

The way you phrase these statements is a question of personal taste, style and judgement. As you gain experience, you'll find it gets easier.

High expectations are a powerful tool in gaining good behaviour and hard work from your students, because they demonstrate your faith in the potential of every single member of your class. There's an excellent example of this in the film *Dangerous Minds*. The teacher (Michelle Pfeiffer) begins her first lesson by telling her class of disaffected students that they all have a grade 'A'. When this statement is greeted with shouts of derision, she explains that they *do* all have an 'A', it's just that it's up to them whether they keep it or lose it.

To establish your expectations effectively:

✓ **Use clear, specific statements**: give positive targets of what you want the students to do, rather than negative statements about what you don't.

✓ **Describe the behaviour:** when you ask for silent attention, be clear what it looks like – eyes to the front, sitting still, listening to what is said. Be clear in your own mind what your expectation looks like, and let your students know too.

✓ **Discuss them:** spend time talking with (not at) the class about what you want. Ask your students what acceptable behaviour is and why it's needed.

✓ **Not too many at once:** don't give out long lists of demands in your first lesson – your students won't retain them. Work out your key expectations and get these in place first.

✓ **Refer back to them:** talk about your expectations repeatedly – at the end of the session, at the start of the next, when you see someone meeting them. Revisit them every time you meet.

✓ **Use a 'drip-feed' approach:** introduce further expectations as appropriate over the next few meetings. Link your expectations with an activity – for instance, the first time you do group work, establish the behaviour that you expect from students.

✓ **Match your phrasing to the group:** adapt your explanation to fit the age/attitude of your students. Be as firm as you can get away with in your particular age group. Don't terrify them, but don't come across as a soft touch either. With young students, be very clear and simple; with older ones, take a more subtle approach.

✓ **Model what you're after:** as well as *telling* the students what you want, you absolutely must *show* them by your own behaviour. If you've asked for silence, don't then go and talk over them!

Establishing the pattern of your lessons/days

The first lesson is a stressful experience for both teacher and students, because there are so many unknown factors. You've not yet built up a relationship with the group, and theoretically 'anything could happen'. To make the situation feel more controlled and manageable, and to help your students feel secure, you must establish a clear structure or pattern. At secondary or further education level, this means creating a pattern to each lesson; in early years or primary, it means finding a structure for your days. Do this as soon as you can and make a start in your first meeting.

You can establish a pattern for many different aspects of your hourly or daily routine. Consider the following questions to help you work out the best structure for you and your class:

- How do your students enter at the start of the lesson/day?
- Where do you stand when the students are entering?
- What are you doing while the students come in?
- What do the students do once they're in the room?
- How does the session start?
- At what point during your time together do you take the register?
- How much talking is allowed during individual activities?
- How does the session finish?
- How do the students leave the room?

As you can see, there are lots of individual decisions to make before you can fully establish the 'pattern' of your lessons. Probably the best way to illustrate what I mean by 'pattern' is to give an example. Below you'll find an account of one way of doing things in a lower-secondary English lesson, lasting for one hour. I've given a commentary to show why the teacher uses this pattern, or set of structures.

9.00 a.m. – the bell goes. Mr Charman checks that he has everything ready, then goes to wait outside the room, closing the door behind him.

Comment: the teacher begins the lesson by standing outside the room, with the door closed. This creates a physical and psychological barrier between the students and his space.

9.03 a.m. – the students arrive in dribs and drabs. Mr Charman stays waiting for them at the door, arms folded. He appears relaxed but ready. As they turn up, he calmly directs individuals to line up, in single file, until everyone arrives.

Comment: the pattern for lessons is being set. The class will line up outside the room until they have all arrived, a useful classroom management technique for this age group. As yet, Mr Charman has not addressed the whole class. He is waiting to do this until most of the students have arrived.

9.07 a.m. – Mr Charman looks very deliberately at his watch and clears his throat. He is now ready to begin. He gets the students silent, then talks to them briefly about what they should do as they enter the room. He wants bags under desks, pencil cases out, and then facing the front, ready to listen.

Comment: the teacher has been lenient with the time, so as not to set up confrontations at the start of his first lesson. He'll explain his exact requirements for future punctuality once the class is settled.

9.12 a.m. – the class are settled in their seats. Mr Charman waits for a moment until they fall silent. He begins by explaining how his lessons will run. He sets his three main boundaries and makes it clear why these are important. He alludes to his encyclopaedic knowledge of the school sanctions policy, in case anyone might choose to misbehave.

Comment: although the teacher will normally move quickly into the teaching and learning part of his lessons, during this first meeting he needs to establish his expectations. He makes his boundaries very clear, while his students are at their most receptive.

9.17 a.m. – Mr Charman reminds the class of his expectation of silent attention when someone is talking. He explains to the class that he likes to start his lessons by checking who is present. He tells the students what the sanction will be for lateness. He then takes the register.

Comment: taking the register at the start of lessons is a matter of personal taste and the teaching situation you're in. In some schools or with some age groups, it would not be sensible or useful to aim to do this – better to get the students going on some activities first.

9.20 a.m. – next Mr Charman needs to sort out exercise books. He explains to the students that, when they get their book, they should write their name, subject, class and teacher on the front. He writes this information up on his interactive whiteboard.

Comment: in your first few lessons, be very clear about these details – what do they write, how do they write it, what do they write with? Establish what you expect early on.

9.22 a.m. – having finished his explanation, Mr Charman pre-empts any problems with a lack of writing materials, by asking for 'hands up' from anyone who doesn't have a pen. Three students have turned up without their equipment. As he moves around the room handing pens to these students, he tells them that this must be a one-off. He explains that, in future, anyone arriving without a pen will get an automatic sanction. He asks for two volunteers to hand out the new books and chooses students who have been listening really well. He also sets a time limit of 3 minutes to get this task done, so that they can get on with the 'lesson proper'.

Comment: think ahead about potential issues that might crop up. Notice here how Mr Charman thinks ahead about those who might not have pens. He also chooses volunteers (a reward) who have been following his expectations already. In your first meeting with a class, there's often various bits of 'admin' to get done. Be clear about your exact requirements to save yourself time and stress.

9.25 a.m. – all the students have got their books sorted. Now Mr Charman brings out five items – a pack of playing cards, a football scarf, a CD, a trowel and a map of Spain. He explains that he wants to get to know them a bit better. Each of these items have a close connection to his life – what do they think those connections could be? They discuss this in pairs and give some suggestions as a whole class. Next he asks them to turn to the person sitting next to them, and talk about five items that have a connection to *their* lives.

Comment: Mr Charman is setting up a quick activity that will give him an insight into what his students are 'into'. He also wants to give them a brief insight into who he is. By using engaging resources to start the activity, he hooks them into it. He understands they have been sitting listening for a while, so he uses talk partners to liven things up.

9.30 a.m. – Mr Charman asks for hands up (establishing this expectation), from anyone who would like to explain what they chose and why. He gets the class to share their ideas, all the time reinforcing that they must wait for silent attention before they address the class.

Comment: the teacher gets the whole class to share their ideas, while at the same time reinforcing his expectations of their behaviour.

9.40 a.m. – Mr Charman sets a brief written task: 'My Life in Five Items'. Before they begin, he clarifies how written tasks will be done: title, date, neat handwriting, care with spelling, and so on.

Comment: Mr Charman wants to see a short sample of each student's writing, so he sets them a quick written task to finish off the lesson. The pattern of his lessons has been set. He will start by explaining the aim of the lesson; there will be plenty of variety in the type of tasks chosen; he will keep his students' interest throughout.

9.53 a.m. – Mr Charman stops the class, gets silence, and then explains the pattern for the end of lessons. The students will write their homework down and clear away equipment one table at a time.

Comment: the teacher has left plenty of time so that the end of his first lesson is calm and well managed.

9.57 a.m. – the students have put the resources away. Mr Charman gets silence, then asks them to stand behind their chairs. He praises them for the excellent work they have done.

Comment: by ending early, Mr Charman has time to praise his students. He sets up a good feeling about this first lesson together. He also has time to host a plenary, to make clear his expectations about homework, or answer any last-minute queries.

10.00 a.m. – when the bell goes, Mr Charman lets the best-behaved and hardest-working students go first, praising them as they leave.

Comment: to finish, the teacher shows how to earn the 'reward' of going first – by working hard and behaving sensibly. The students leave with a good first impression of a well-structured, well-managed lesson.

Learning names

From the moment we're born, our names are a fundamental part of what makes us who we are. Even if you don't particularly like your name, it's still inextricably linked with you and your interactions with the world. Learning and using names is a very powerful way to build relationships and manage behaviour. By using someone's name, you show your awareness of the individuals in your class, and you demonstrate respect for those individuals. As any supply teacher will attest, when you're trying to control students' behaviour, you are at a great disadvantage if you do not know their names.

Once you know names, you can:

✓ Get a student's attention
✓ Use them to personalize a reward
✓ Highlight a student who's working well
✓ Use them to give a sanction
✓ Pass them on to the relevant senior member of staff
✓ Build positive relationships.

Unfortunately, there's no magical short cut to learning names. It's clearly easier in the early years, and at primary school, where you work mainly with one smallish group of students. However, at secondary or further education levels, you could teach literally hundreds of different students. If that's the case for you, use every technique you can think of to make the process quicker and smoother. Incorporate some or all of the ideas below into your first meeting with the group.

You could:

✓ **Use memory systems**: memory systems are a useful approach for teachers, particularly when learning names. The basic idea is the use of 'hooks' or connections between things (do a search online or see one of Tony Buzan's books for more about different memory techniques). You might have a student called David who looks like a well-known footballer, or a large student named Ben (think 'Big Ben').

✓ **Make notes on your register**: a few subtle annotations on your class list can help you learn names. Make a brief note of any distinguishing characteristics (such as a student who wears glasses).

✓ **Set yourself a target**: faced with a sea of students, the task of learning names seems huge, especially if you teach hundreds of different students. Set yourself a reasonable target: five or so names per lesson. Within a few weeks you should have learnt the names of all your students (or a few days in a primary class).

✓ **Do name games and activities**: spend some time doing name-specific activities in your first couple of lessons. Ask your students to make decorated nameplates to sit on their desks, or to wear sticky name labels. Get them writing an acrostic poem, using the first letters of their names to start each line. Ask them to talk about their names to the class: whether they like it, who chose it, why they were called that, and so on.

✓ **Focus on the quiet ones**: when you're teaching a class with poorly behaved students in it, it is tempting to focus on the troublemakers, learning those names first. As a result, you struggle to learn the names of the quiet students. Focus on getting to know at least one or two quiet students in your first meeting as well.

And of course . . .

✓ **Use a seating plan**: this is a great way of learning names, and it's also useful for keeping control of a class. With a seating plan in place, you send a definite signal about your style – structured, orderly, in charge. You can use 'being allowed to sit where you want' as a reward for consistent good behaviour.

If you're new to teaching, it's tough to get a seating plan in place while dealing with all the other stresses of the first meeting. Unfortunately, if you don't do it in that first lesson, it gets harder to do it later on. There are various different methods for getting a seating plan in place – ask other staff for advice. For instance, you might:

✓ Draw up a plan and stick it on the wall for the students to follow.
✓ Let the students in one by one, seating them as you go.
✓ Ask the students to line up, and then seat themselves, in register order.

If you're not comfortable about getting a seating plan in place in your first lesson, you can still get a student to draw you one up, once the class is seated. Refer to this as you start to learn names.

Reducing the stress of the first meeting

Although the first lesson can be stressful remember that, as yet, the students have formed little or no opinion of you. If you are an old hand at your school, your reputation will precede you, particularly if there are siblings of students you have already taught in the class. If you are a new teacher at the school, you are currently the 'mystery man', an unknown entity, and consequently of great interest. Older students have an uncanny ability to identify (and subsequently to be difficult for) trainee teachers. If that's you, prepare a convincing answer to the question: 'Are you a student teacher?'

If you experience problems in your first lesson, you can find that your confidence drops and defensiveness takes over. If that happens:

✓ **Stay calm and relaxed:** if you get tense and angry, you give your students an incentive to misbehave in future. Breathe deeply, pull yourself together, and stay calm.

✓ **React from the head**: make a conscious decision to react intellectually, rather than emotionally. Don't let your heart win the day – there's simply no point in getting upset or angry.

✓ **Don't get defensive**: remind yourself that it's not personal. If your students 'attack' your lesson by misbehaving, refuse to respond by becoming hostile in return. It's far more useful to stay relentlessly positive.

And if all else fails . . .

✓ **Don't be a perfectionist**: it's not a total disaster if a few students muck around in your first lesson. The world is not going to end. You're not going to get the sack. And you'll learn some valuable lessons from the experience.

3

Key strategies and techniques

How do I gain and keep control?

Before I give you my 'key strategies and techniques' for managing your classroom, it's worth considering why you need to control your students' behaviour in the first place. Obviously, it's important for safety reasons, but actually the main reason good behaviour is needed is so that the students can get on with learning. Understanding how to manage behaviour is not about being some kind of control freak, it's done simply so that you can get on with the job of teaching. The more strategies you have at your disposal to achieve this control, the more confident you will feel. When things are going wrong, you can try one approach after another, until you find something that works.

Controlling a large group of people is difficult in any situation, but when some of your students have no wish to be in school, let alone in your lesson, life can become very difficult indeed. In addition to using the basic techniques described in Chapter 1, you can use various other methods to create and maintain an orderly yet relaxed atmosphere in your classroom. The ten strategies described below are relatively easy to understand and apply, and should cost you little in the way of stress.

1   Wait for silence
2   Make use of cues
3   Give them 'the choice'
4   Be reasonable, but don't reason with them
5   Learn to 'read and respond'
6   Use statements, not questions, and assume compliance
7   Use repetition
8   Set targets and time limits
9   Use humour
10 Put yourself in their shoes.

1. Learn to 'read and respond'

As well as being made up of individuals, a class is also an entity in its own right. There are days when it is easy to manage, others when it is a nightmare to handle. There are many factors that can affect the behaviour of a class, or of the individuals within that group.

These factors include:

- The time of day
- The day of the week
- The weather (watch out for windy or rainy days)
- The presence or absence of certain individuals
- What happened in the previous lesson
- Any incidents at break or lunchtime
- The teaching space you are working in
- The topic area you are covering
- The activities that you are using
- The mood of the teacher
- Outside events (e.g. a local football match on TV that night).

You can hype up a class, and equally you can calm it down. Sometimes you'll catch yourself getting the students overexcited, and you'll automatically take measures to bring down the excitement levels. This effect is particularly vivid with young children: even the way your voice sounds is enough to get some classes hyped up. You can also have exactly the same effect on individual students, particularly when you are dealing with their behaviour.

The ability to 'read and respond' to a class or an individual, by adapting what you do instantly, is a subtle skill to learn. It involves using the flexibility discussed in the first chapter. This technique comes more easily with experience, and also as you get to know your class and the people within it. To 'read and respond', you need to:

✓ Make on-the-spot judgements during the lesson.
✓ Base these judgements both on how students are responding to the activities that you're doing, and also on how your approaches to behaviour are working.
✓ Adapt or even throw away a lesson activity if it's not working.
✓ Change your behaviour management techniques if necessary.
✓ Be particularly flexible on days when there are already high levels of tension in the class or with particular individuals.

This technique is especially important for supply and cover teachers. It's also vital if you have a student with a 'short fuse' in your class. Don't lower your standards, but use your professional judgement to make decisions about the right balance between consistency and flexibility.

2. Wait for silence

Waiting for silence is one of the most important techniques a teacher can use to encourage and enhance learning. When I say 'wait for silence', I don't mean get your students silent and then talk at them endlessly. What I mean is *when you need to talk to the whole class* you should not address the students until they are completely silent and fully focused on you (or on whoever is speaking). This applies at the start of the day or lesson, for instance when taking the register, and also at any time when you wish to talk to the class (whatever age the students are).

When you get silent attention:

✓ You send a clear message: the learning is important and you will not allow it to be jeopardized.

✓ The students can hear your explanations or instructions.
✓ It shows respect to the speaker and is polite.
✓ Listening well is a skill that many students need to practise.

Remember, if you give up, and let the students talk over you, you are basically saying: 'Go ahead and talk, I don't mind.' When working with very young children, you can only hope for a few minutes of silence at a time. With adults, you can ask for more (although even they have a threshold and will drift off if you don't spice things up with other approaches). A great rule of thumb, in most situations, is to speak for a maximum of about **'their age plus two'**, i.e. 5 minutes for a 3-year-old, 10 minutes for an 8-year-old, and so on. Of course, that is not to say that you *have* to use up all that time with talking.

In your quest to get silence, it is better to use non-verbal, rather than verbal, techniques. These create less stress for you and add less noise to your classroom. They also give a sense of control and confidence. There is little more ineffective than the teacher shouting over a noisy class 'Be quiet! Be quiet!'. You can find some age-specific strategies for getting silent attention in Chapters 11 and 12. Here are a few approaches that you can adapt to suit most ages:

✓ **The force of your personality**: if the class is reasonably well behaved, try standing with your arms folded, looking ready or, if necessary, mean. Hold your nerve and refuse to begin speaking until there is silence. If this technique is going to work (and it might not), it will do so within a couple of minutes.
✓ **The power of the pause**: in teaching, you quickly learn that there's a lot of waiting around. When you are in the middle of talking to the class, and an individual begins to talk, use a pause to indicate that you are waiting for silence. At first it can feel as though you are wasting lots of time, but eventually you will train your students in the behaviour you want.
✓ **Visual cues**: add a visual element to your pauses by using an egg timer. Every time you have to wait for the class, turn the timer over so that some sand runs through. Once the students fall silent, turn the egg timer on its side so that the sand remains

in place. This gives a visual indication of time wasted. You could insist that the students 'earn' this time back, perhaps through working in silence for a while.

✓ **The non-verbal 'silence command'**: A pre-agreed non-verbal signal is a useful way to achieve silence. It is essential in some subjects or situations (for instance, in PE or drama, where the students may be engaged in a noisy activity or spread around an open space). A group of young children could be engrossed in a game and less conscious of non-verbal signals – in these instances, use a sound instead. Train your class to respond quickly to your chosen signal, practising and praising the students until they get it right. Turn it into a game or challenge, to make it fun for younger students to join in. With older students, try turning it into a kind of shared joke. I even use this technique when working with adults. Your 'silence commands' might be:
  - Blowing a whistle or ringing a bell
  - Rapping three times on a desk
  - Clapping in a pattern, which the students must copy
  - Raising a hand – everyone else must stop and raise theirs
  - Sitting in your 'silent seat'
  - Doing a little boogie (embarrassing but gets their attention).

✓ **The well-chosen phrase**: with some classes a verbal cue for silence is effective. Pitch your voice at a fairly quiet volume. Here are some age-specific phrases you could try:
  - 3–5 years: 'Let's see fingers on lips, everyone, that's great!'
  - 5+ years: 'Looking this way and listening carefully, thanks.'
  - 11+ years: 'I need complete silence before I continue.'
  - 15+ years: 'C'mon guys, everyone listening now, please.'
  - Any age: 'Let's have silence in 5 . . . 4 . . . 3 . . . 2 . . . 1.'

✓ **The 'broken record' technique**: if your students don't respond immediately to your well-chosen phrase, this technique is fun and effective. All you do is repeat your phrase over and over again, perhaps stopping midway through, until the students finally get what you are saying.

Talk about your expectation of silent attention in your first lesson with a class. Get them thinking about why this boundary is so important. Model the behaviour you're after – listen really carefully to your students when they are talking, and try never to talk over a class.

If you find that you simply can't get your class silent, particularly at the start of a lesson, then think laterally to get around the problem. Perhaps you should plunge them straight into an engaging starter activity instead? Maybe you could get a student to help you mark off names on the register? It's better even to write messages to your class on your whiteboard, than to talk over them if they don't intend to listen.

3. Make use of cues

A lot of teacher stress is caused by fairly low-level misbehaviour – students calling out answers rather than putting their hands up, or starting an activity before you've finished explaining it. The idea behind the use of cues is to get the students doing the behaviour you do want, rather than letting them behave incorrectly first, then having to tell them off. You can use cues for any behaviour that is repeated regularly, and they can be verbal or non-verbal. Cues often change over time, becoming a form of shorthand understood by all. Here are a couple of examples to show you what I mean:

✓ **Answering questions**: start any whole-class question with the phrase: 'Put your hand up if you can tell me . . .'. By specifying the behaviour you want (hands up), you anticipate and overcome the incorrect response (calling out). This can gradually be abbreviated to 'Hands up' or just a slight raise of your hand.

✓ **Giving instructions**: some keen students want to start work before you finish giving the instructions; others don't want to start at all. Use the phrase 'When I say "go" I want you to . . .' to pre-empt this. Once you've finish your explanation, set the class off to work by saying '3, 2, 1, go.' Again, this becomes a shorthand, with the question 'Did I say go yet?' making clear what the cue will be.

4. Give them 'the choice'

We cannot actually force our students to behave – we can only make it seem like the best of all possible options. Ideally, we want them to take responsibility for their own actions, and for the consequences of those actions. This is important in creating a positive and effective environment for learning. It is also vital in setting people up for their lives beyond education, when the choices they make about behaviour become potentially that much more crucial ('Should I go with my friends to burgle that house or not?').

This is where the technique of 'the choice' comes in. There are essentially two choices: either the students do as you ask, or they accept the consequences of a refusal to comply. You want to get on with teaching and learning – if their behaviour makes that impossible, you utilize the rules of the organization to impose a consequence. This is only fair on the majority who *do* want to learn. If we make the choices and consequences simple and clear enough, this can prevent misbehaviour occurring or escalating. It also encourages students to consider and change their negative behaviours, to avoid unwelcome consequences in the future.

'The choice' helps you depersonalize a range of tricky situations, because it puts responsibility in the hands of the student. It is up to her to decide how she wishes to behave, and which consequences she is willing to receive. Your role is that of 'police officer' – applying the code of conduct of the place where you work.

When using 'the choice':

✓ State the behaviour you require.
✓ Make clear the positive benefits of doing as you ask.
✓ Make clear the consequences of refusing to comply.
✓ Give the student a short time to consider her decision.
✓ If she decides not to comply, apply the consequences.
✓ Aim to sound disappointed, rather than vengeful when doing this.

Let's look at a couple of examples of a teacher using 'the choice', to see how it works:

Reception-age students

Hafiz is pushing other children in the role-play area. The teacher has just seen him grab a doll from Tiffany and she is now crying.

Teacher: Hafiz, I need you to play nicely and stop pushing the other children. Give the doll back to Tiffany right now please.

Hafiz: [*holding it tight*] Won't! It's mine.

Teacher: Hafiz, give it back to Tiffany now, or I'll have to take it away and you won't be able to play in here anymore. That would be a shame, wouldn't it?

Hafiz: No, I won't give it back. I want to play with it.

Teacher: [*deciding to use a distraction to back up 'the choice'*] Oh look! Tiffany's got a buggy for the doll. Pop it in the buggy, Hafiz, and then come and do some painting with me.

At this point Hafiz will either do as he's asked, or the teacher will take the doll from him and lead him away from the area.

Students of 13+ years

Sandra is in a terrible mood. As she enters the classroom, she shoves her way past a group of girls, pushing one student to the floor.

Teacher: Sandra! That's unacceptable behaviour. [*Pointing to the door*] I want you to come outside with me right now, please, so we can discuss this and you can make an apology to Ana.

Sandra: Nah, I won't. Are you gonna make me?

Teacher: Sandra. You have a choice. Come outside with me right now so we can sort this out. If you refuse, I will have to send for a senior member of staff to remove you from my lesson. And I really don't want to do that. I'll wait for you outside while you decide.

Again, at this point, Sandra will either comply or the teacher will have to follow through with the consequences.

5. *Be reasonable, but don't reason with them*

I was given this tip by a headteacher in a Scottish school, and it struck me as a wonderful summary of an effective and balanced approach to teacher/student (and indeed parent/child) relationships. So long as you are reasonable with your students, and you don't have unrealistic expectations about how they will work or behave, then there is no need to actually reason with them over what you do ask them to do.

Here are some examples of how this might work with different age groups:

Early years
It's perfectly reasonable to insist they don't paint on the walls. *So long as you don't* get cross about the odd splash on the floor.

Primary
It's perfectly reasonable to have silence to explain an activity. *So long as you don't* take 15 minutes to explain it.

Secondary
It's perfectly reasonable to ask students to write in silence. *So long as you don't* expect them to write for hours at a time.

Further education
It's perfectly reasonable to insist that mobile phones are kept in bags. *So long as you don't* remove a phone from a student whose parent is in hospital.

When problem behaviour is challenged, students often try to drag you into a discussion, rather than accepting responsibility for what they did. Some students are very clever at deflecting the teacher's challenge, and it is important to learn to stick to your guns, rather than be drawn into endless debates about 'whose fault it was' or 'why I can't do this work'. The 'being reasonable' part of the equation is tricky to manage – you need to make difficult decisions about the right balance to strike. Set high standards, and expect the very best, but be realistic as well. If you are too authoritarian with your demands, confrontations and difficulties arise. Similarly, if you're too reasonable and relaxed, students will take advantage.

6. *Use statements, not questions, and assume compliance*

It's a common mistake: asking rhetorical questions to manage behaviour. Here's the classic scenario:

Student:	You're a 'f*****g b***h'!
Teacher:	[*horrified*] What did you say?
Student:	I said, 'you're a f*****g b***h!'

I suspect it might be a matter of habit – we frequently use questions in our work, so we get used to this vocal style. To help you overcome the habit, a really useful rule of thumb is: 'never ask a question if you don't want to get an answer'.

Instead, use statements about what you want, rather than questions about what you don't. This is much more helpful for your students – you state what they should be doing, rather than complaining about what they are not. It also gives the impression of someone who knows what she wants, and who has confidence that the children will comply. Of course, in some situations a question is appropriate and you want to receive an answer. For instance, asking a child: 'Is there something the matter today?' might be a good starting point for a discussion about behaviour.

Here are a few examples of questions, and how they might be rephrased as statements:

- ✓ 'Why aren't you doing the work?' becomes 'I want you to get on with the activity now, so you can leave on time.'
- ✓ 'Why are you being so silly?' becomes 'I want you to sit properly on your chair and focus on the learning, thanks.'
- ✓ 'Why aren't you listening?' becomes 'Everyone looking this way and listening in silence, thanks.'

When you're making these positive statements about what you want, you can also use a technique called 'assumed compliance'. All that is meant by this term is that you say 'thanks' (you assume they'll do it) rather than 'please' (you're hoping they will). If you use these two techniques simultaneously, it gives the added benefit of making you sound like a teacher who is very positive, certain and confident about getting what she wants.

7. Use repetition

Much of the time, when we say something, we expect it to be heard and understood the first time around. This is not necessarily a sensible expectation to have, and it can lead to unnecessary misunderstandings and confrontations. Classrooms and other teaching spaces can be noisy and confusing places for our students: there might be many different reasons why they do not respond immediately to your directions. Here are some of the times when you might usefully use repetition with your students:

✓ To get their attention before you give an instruction
✓ To ensure they are listening if you need to warn them about a potential sanction
✓ Because they might not hear your instructions the first time you give them
✓ To clarify any possible misunderstandings and make your wishes perfectly clear
✓ To reinforce your instructions and make it clear that they must be followed.

Repetition is particularly helpful when you have to sanction a student. In this situation, you might repeat:

✓ The name of the student, to get her attention
✓ The instruction you have given or the behaviour you want (ask the student to repeat this, to check for understanding)
✓ The options for avoiding a sanction
✓ The sanction you are giving, if the student fails to comply.

Here's an example of how you might use repetition to deal with behaviour. Alice is chatting to her friends instead of working.

Teacher: Alice. [*The teacher waits, there is no response.*]
Teacher: Alice. I'd like you to look at me and listen, thanks.

Alice: What, Miss? [*She is still looking at her friends.*]
Teacher: Alice. I said I want you to look at me and listen.

Finally, she turns around and looks at the teacher.

Teacher: Thank you, Alice. Right, I want you to get on with
                your work right now. No more talking, please.
Alice: Okay then.

She turns back, but continues chatting.

Teacher: Oh Alice?
Alice: Yeah?
Teacher: Could you repeat what I just said? What was my
                instruction?
Alice: To get on with my work and stop talking.
Teacher: Good. I'm glad you understand. I'd *hate* to have to
                give you a detention. [*Smiles to suggest it is a serious
                possibility.*]

8. Set targets and time limits

Learning always works best when you've got clear objectives – a
specific target at which to aim. Targets can help you harness our
natural sense of competition: perhaps against others, but more
importantly against our own previous best. Having a clear amount
to achieve, within a set time frame, helps create a sense of urgency
and pace to the work. It gives a clear structure – something definite
towards which the students can work. Targets also help your less
able children feel a sense of achievement. When the teacher asks
the class to work in groups to find five ideas in 3 minutes, even
the least able should be able to contribute to this task.

You might use a whole range of different targets: a target for
how many words or answers the students must complete; a time
for completing the activity; a target for improving behaviour, such
as staying in seats. When setting targets, use the following tips to
help you get it right:

✓ Make sure your targets suit the students: don't make them too hard to achieve, nor conversely too easy.

✓ Keep targets short and specific for maximum impact – five words, 3 minutes, and so on.

✓ Add visual prompts to aid understanding, for instance holding up a hand to show 'five words'.

✓ Use your voice, or even some music, to create a sense of pace and urgency. Try the theme tune from *Mission Impossible* or the opening music from *Countdown*.

✓ Use language to enhance your students' motivation levels: words such as 'competition', 'prize' and 'challenge'.

✓ Make sure any rewards offered for completion of targets are ones that really appeal to the group or the individual.

To illustrate this technique further, here are some examples:

A whole-group target for behaviour – early years

'Right, children, I've got a very special challenge for you today. Today I want everyone to follow our golden rule – walk, don't run. And for everyone who manages to follow that rule, I've got these fantastic stickers to go on your shoes. Hands up who thinks they can do that!'

An individual target for learning – upper primary

'Okay, Arwel. What I want you to do today is to concentrate on putting full stops in your writing, but they must be in the right place. Don't worry too much about spelling, because today we're going to focus on the punctuation. And if you do manage to put all the full stops in, you can choose one of these fantastic stickers.'

A whole-class target for learning – lower secondary

'Right. Today we're going to have a competition. As you can see, I've written ten questions up on the board about the work we did last lesson. The first person to answer all ten, in full sentences, can leave first when the bell goes. Ready, steady, go!'

An individual target for behaviour – further education

'Could I have a quick word, Chris? Look, I know we've not been getting on that well, but I was hoping you'd do something for me today? The college has told me that I've got to fill out one of these yellow slips if I hear anyone

*swearing in our lesson. Could you help me keep an ear out for any bad
language? Oh and obviously I don't want to have to fill one out for you,
so your challenge today is not to say a single swear word. Do you think
you can do that?'*

9. Use humour

Humour is incredibly powerful in the classroom. Teachers who
make their students laugh, and who can laugh with them when
appropriate, inevitably form good relationships with their classes.
Of course there are times when you can't see the funny side. On a
Monday morning/Friday afternoon, when you're tired, hungover,
getting a cold or are just plain cranky, you might not feel in the
mood for a stand-up comedy routine. But if you can take a fun
approach to the job, and make the work and the lessons seem like
light relief, this will definitely help you to manage behaviour.

Alongside its beneficial effects on your students, humour:

✓ Offers a respite from the tension that can build up in a poorly
   behaved class
✓ Makes your work fun for yourself and your students
✓ Helps you stay relaxed and rational
✓ Helps you avoid defensiveness.

Use humour to dissipate the threat of low-level personal insults: be
clear that you refuse to take this kind of stuff seriously and your
students will soon give up on doing this. With older students, you
can turn an insult on its head by agreeing with what the student
has said. So, if a student says, 'Your hair looks really stupid like
that, Miss', you might answer (deadpan), 'Yes, I know, I'm planning to sue my hairdresser'.

Learn to laugh at yourself when you make a mistake, for
instance tripping over or saying something daft. Students love a
teacher who is willing to be self-deprecating. It's a good way of
undermining the image of teacher as authoritarian figure, and it
shows that you don't take yourself too seriously.

Generally speaking, it is best to avoid sarcasm, although I appreciate that it offers a way of letting off steam in stressful situations.
You should also avoid laughing at, and encouraging other children

to laugh at, individual students. Your 'class clowns' might enjoy the attention, but some shy children may be mortified to hear their peers laughing at them.

10. Put yourself in their shoes

When you're dealing with persistent misbehaviour, it is easy to lose your sense of perspective. You may begin to feel that students are deliberately being awkward, and even that they have a personal vendetta against you. In turn, this leads to overreactions to what is actually relatively minor misbehaviour. Develop the ability to step outside yourself, and to view what happens from your students' perspective. Become a reflective teacher, constantly engaged in a process of self-analysis. This in turn will feed into every aspect of your practice.

When an activity doesn't seem to be working, or the students start misbehaving, put yourself in their shoes to try to work out why:

✓ Is there too much listening and not enough doing?
✓ Is the concept too hard for the class to grasp?
✓ Do the students find this particular topic area boring?
✓ Is this work too easy for the group?

Sometimes you can't do much about the situation – they have to get through a particularly tough bit of learning. But at least if you put yourself in their shoes, you can understand why they might fidget. Similarly, you can analyse your own teaching by using this approach. If your students often become confrontational with you when you try to discipline them, step back and view the way that you deal with behaviour from the outside. Are you saying or doing something to exacerbate the situation? Are there external factors at work?

When you take on the adult role of 'teacher', make sure you don't lose sight of what it was like to be the student. Sometimes your students will mess around just because it's human nature to do so. Winding up your teacher has been a classic childhood pursuit, ever since schools were first invented. Even adults regularly try it on the INSET Days that I run.

PART TWO

The Teacher and the Teaching

4

The effective teacher

The learning process

Becoming an effective teacher is a learning process that starts the first time you set foot in a classroom, and is one that should never really end, no matter how many years of experience you have in the job. There are many different facets to the effective teacher – skilled verbal and non-verbal communication, the ability to manage the class and the classroom space, an understanding of how to match teaching style to a particular situation, the knowledge to plan for and deliver high-quality lessons. All of these qualities can be learnt and developed, and each of us will benefit from working on particular areas of our own practice. In this chapter I look at those aspects of effective teaching that are connected to the teacher as a person and a communicator, rather than as an educator. (See Chapter 7 on p. 101 for advice on planning and delivering the curriculum.)

It's probably fair to say that some people are born teachers – they have a natural ability to engage with and inspire others, to transmit ideas or knowledge, and to control the behaviour of groups of people. To an extent, this is about charisma, self-confidence and the power of personality. For these natural teachers, the skills and attitudes described in this chapter might come instinctively. But we can't all be born teachers, and in any case it's the willingness to learn and develop that is important, and not the point from which you start that process.

The teacher as role model

At first, the idea of being a role model takes a bit of getting used to. Sometimes you are a role model simply by virtue of your age, gender, subject area or social/cultural background. You might be the only male teacher working in your primary school, or the only female physics teacher in your local area. But the teacher as role model is about much more than that. It's about offering a consistent model of appropriate behaviour and attitudes, often for those who lack this outside of the educational environment. Some of our most difficult students are used to adults behaving aggressively: it takes time for them to realize that there are other ways of interacting with the world.

Young people model what they see, and it is worth keeping this in mind when you are frustrated by the behaviour of some of your students (of whatever age). If a child is brought up in a house where every other word is a swear word, it is likely that he will bring this language into school. But if they respect you, your students will want to emulate you. They might copy your behaviour and your ways of relating to people; they might study the subject you teach to A level and beyond, because you have inspired them to love it as much as you do.

One of the key ways we can model good behaviour for our students is to treat them as we would wish to be treated ourselves, i.e. politely and with respect. We might like to think that being polite would be a relatively straightforward strategy to adopt and maintain. However, when faced with the stress caused by persistent aggression or rudeness, it is all too easy to get sucked into a similar attitude. Before you know it, you are making rude comments and being sarcastic – something you would probably never do in your life outside of school. Irritation is often an entirely understandable response, but at the same time it's not helpful.

A relentlessly polite manner helps you:

✓ Defuse difficult situations
✓ Set an appropriate example of good behaviour
✓ Show other students that it is possible to stay calm when dealing with frustrating situations

✓ Stay 'in the right' and show that the aggressive student is 'in the wrong'.

The scenarios below show the teacher offering two very different models of behaviour. In the first instance, notice how the comments very quickly become a 'tit-for-tat' battle of rudeness. In the second, watch the teacher staying relaxed and defusing every rude comment that is made.

✗ *Reacting 'in kind'*

Teacher:	Jason, get on with your work and stop causing problems.
Jason:	No I won't. This work is stupid and your lessons are boring.
Teacher:	No, Jason, your attitude is stupid, not the work.
Jason:	Don't call me stupid, you old cow.
Teacher:	How dare you call me an old cow! Right, you're in detention.
Jason:	Oh yeah? Well I'm not coming. I hate you.
Teacher:	And I hate you too. [*Shouting*] NOW GET ON WITH THE WORK!

✓ *Modelling polite behaviour*

Teacher:	Jason, please could you get on with your work now.
Jason:	No I won't. This work is stupid and your lessons are boring!
Teacher:	I'm sorry you feel that way. I do try to make them as interesting as I can. Now please get on with the work.
Jason:	No I won't! You're an old cow!
Teacher:	That's rather harsh. I'm not that old, am I, Jason? I'm not even thirty yet.
Jason:	[*totally confused by this response*] Huh?
Teacher:	Now please get on with the work. You have 10 minutes to finish. I'd love to see how well you can do.

Effective verbal and non-verbal communication

When you step in front of a class, you take on a role or character to communicate with your audience, just as an actor does when he walks out onto the stage. Your students are taking their cues about how to behave at least partly from the way that you use your voice and your body. If you can communicate confidence and certainty, this helps you achieve high status in the teacher/student relationship. If students look up to you and respect you, they are consequently more likely to behave.

It is important to think carefully about the physical aspects of your teaching, particularly if you are not naturally a confident person. Remember that you don't have to feel confident inside, you just need to communicate a confident persona through your verbal and non-verbal signals. Right from the start, your students are examining your teacher persona (often subconsciously), to decide how they are going to behave.

Using your voice

The teacher's voice is a tool, an instrument that must be used every single day of our working lives. It is vital that we learn to take good care of our vocal instruments – we only have one and we cannot send it away to be repaired. Some teachers will have been trained in good vocal technique (although by no means all). It's certainly easy to pick up bad habits along the way. Make sure that you:

✓ Maintain good posture, particularly when speaking.
✓ Stand upright with your shoulders, neck and chin relaxed.
✓ Use your diaphragm to speak, not your neck muscles.
✓ Keep well hydrated throughout the teaching day.

If you are unsure about good voice usage, or if you regularly lose your voice, ask that you get some quality vocal training.

Your voice and your students

Your voice says a lot about you to your students: it has a powerful impact on their perceptions of you. We all have our own vocal 'style' or personality, which tells others a lot about us as individuals. Think for a moment about the voices of some high-profile figures: where a vocal sound grates or irritates you, this makes you feel negative about the person generally. On the other hand, a beautiful speaking or singing voice helps to create a positive feeling about someone.

The sound of your voice gives people clues about how you are feeling. When faced with a stressful situation, our voices very easily betray our emotions, becoming louder, or cracking under pressure. Your voice offers your students a clear indication of your inner state, and they respond to the signals given through the way that you sound. The secret is for you to be in control: if you need to change the sound of your voice, this should be a conscious decision, rather than being done as a result of stress. You might *feel* angry and bad tempered, but you can *sound* calm and controlled. Keep those negative emotions to yourself if you possibly can.

While you won't want to completely change the way you speak between the normal world and the classroom, it is important to understand how your voice impacts on your ability to manage behaviour. High quality verbal communication:

✓ Helps you develop good relationships with your students
✓ Allows you to teach in a more engaging way
✓ Helps your students learn more effectively
✓ Encourages them to behave better
✓ Protects your voice and prevents it from getting damaged.

There are three main aspects of voice usage that you can adapt and develop. These are: volume, tone and pace.

Volume

It is tough for teachers to achieve and sustain the right volume levels. Although we would hope that we could just 'talk normally' to our students, all the stresses and strains of the typical classroom situation mean that this is often hard to maintain. Getting the right balance in your volume levels is very important in managing behaviour. It helps you show respect for your students and demonstrate emotional self-control; it also helps you teach in a way that allows understanding.

Shouting usually indicates a loss of emotional control, and some students will enjoy this reaction. It's damaging for your voice, and it rarely has any direct impact on misbehaviour. It also signals an 'old-school' approach that is out of sync with modern approaches to education. Remember, some students (typically the well-behaved ones you want to encourage) may feel scared if you shout at them. However, that is not to say you should never raise your voice. If you normally talk with a low volume level, raising your voice slightly gives a powerful impact. Combine this with a sharp tone and you can send a strong message of disapproval with relatively little effort.

To get volume levels right, and to avoid the urge to shout:

✓ Remember – the quieter you are, the quieter your students have to be to hear you. Don't overdo it and whisper, though, as a forced whisper can hurt your voice.
✓ Aim for a conversational volume level: stay alert to the way your emotional state affects the sound of your voice.
✓ When you feel yourself getting wound up, pause for a few seconds to regain self-control before you continue to speak. Breathe deeply and deliberately lower your volume levels.
✓ Learn to 'throw' your voice like an actor to an audience. Imagine the sound as a physical entity – a stone for example – and 'throw' it towards the class.
✓ Talking loudly can be a matter of habit. Listen to yourself regularly during lessons, doing a check on whether your volume level is just right.
✓ To bring down your volume, imagine turning down the sound on a stereo. Lower the sound by about half – you'll be surprised how quietly you can talk and still be heard.
✓ Take acoustics into account. If you teach in different spaces, adapt volume levels as appropriate. The empty space in halls and gyms makes your voice echo; a crowded classroom muffles sound.

✓ When you talk to an individual about his behaviour, get close and speak quietly, so no one else can hear.
✓ When you raise your voice, make it a conscious decision. Do it from a position of emotional control, rather than as an angry and instinctive reaction.

As you learn to retain self-control, this helps with your vocal technique as well, because the sound comes from the diaphragm muscles rather than from tension in the throat.

Tone

Tone is great for adding interest and excitement to your teaching. It helps you engage with your students, because it gives them clues and cues about your emotional state. There are many subtle ways you can adapt and vary your teacher 'character' by using different tones. A range of tones helps you signal a range of thoughts, feelings, reactions and responses to your students. The more you use tone, the more you use your face and body as you teach. A deadpan voice gives a feeling of disengagement and tends to create a flat or lifeless facial expression. An animated voice, full of tone, lights up the face and eyes and creates a sense of connection with your students.

The younger the students you teach, the more tone you can and should put into your voice. If you teach students whose first language is not English, an exaggerated tone with lots of emphasis and facial expressions will help them understand what you are saying. Use a lighter touch with older students: as we age we start to interpret excessive tone as being rather patronizing.

Some useful tones for managing behaviour include:

✓ **Wonder**: put a tone of wonder and interest into your voice to help you engage a class. You can also use this tone when you are particularly pleased with a student's behaviour: 'Oh! I'm so pleased with how you did that.'
✓ **Excitement**: an excited tone helps you give pace and energy to a subject or activity. It also helps you motivate and inspire students in their learning.
✓ **Deadly**: this is a tone that tells your students you are not happy.

It can helpfully be used alongside the 'deadly stare' (see p. 67, 'Using your body'). It is a cold, calculated sound, rather than one of anger. Use it only with older students.

✓ **Disappointed**: when dealing with behaviour, disappointment is one of the most valuable tones of all. Where the class or student respects the teacher, the sense that 'you've let me down' is a very powerful motivator to improve.

Pace

Pace is a fascinating, subtle area of voice usage. Different teachers have their own 'styles' when it comes to the speed at which they like to speak. It's important to adapt the pace you use according to the students you are teaching. With young children, or with those whose language or cognitive skills are not well developed, you need to speak slowly and clearly. On the other hand, with a class who are cynical and disengaged with learning, you need to 'gee them up', using a fast pace to get and keep their interest.

Use a range of different paces during a lesson: this helps you add interest to the learning. Think of words as being like chewing gum – you can stretch them out in your mouth, or shorten them with a quick chomp, as required. It's a question of balance: keep your children engaged but ensure that everyone can understand what you are saying.

A slow pace can:

✓ Calm a student down
✓ Relax a tense situation
✓ Quieten a noisy or overexcited group
✓ Help ensure understanding.

But it can also:

✗ Lead to boredom
✗ Encourage students to switch off
✗ Be perceived as patronizing
✗ Make the teacher appear self-important.

A fast pace can:

✓ Motivate a disengaged class
✓ Perk up a lazy student
✓ Give a lesson energy and forward momentum
✓ Add interest to a dull area of the curriculum.

But it can also:

✗ Hamper proper understanding
✗ Make some students feel stressed
✗ Make the teacher sound harassed
✗ Be wearing on you.

Teacher talk

While on the subject of voice usage, it is worth considering how much you should actually talk at all. Teachers are a bit notorious for loving the sound of their own voices. I know that I personally can be guilty of talking at my students far too much and for far too long. When you speak at a class for more than about 5 or 10 minutes, it is likely that at least some of your students have phased out the sound of your voice, and are contemplating misbehaviour. As far as possible, keep teacher talk to a minimum and active student learning to a maximum.

Listening to someone talk is typically a very passive activity, so when you have to talk for longer periods, find ways to keep it interactive. Intersperse your speaking with the requirement for students to actually do something. For instance:

✓ Make notes
✓ Pick out key words
✓ Draw diagrams
✓ Look at a visual aid
✓ Handle a resource
✓ Answer questions
✓ Talk to a partner
✓ Help you do some demonstrations.

Using your body

There are a whole host of non-verbal signals that teachers give which have an impact on student behaviour. Some of these signals you will use consciously, to help you control your classes. But you will also give subconscious signals at the same time, perhaps betraying a lack of confidence or conveying a sense of stress. The way our students interpret these signals helps them make decisions about how to behave. The secret is to become aware of the signals you send, and to stay in control of them where possible.

It is tempting to use mainly spoken instructions and signals to put across your wishes to a class. However, there are good reasons why non-verbal signals are better:

✓ They send your students a confident message about your status and control.
✓ They require little effort from you, and they do not put a strain on your voice.
✓ You can use them on individuals, without alerting the rest of the class.
✓ They help you avoid giving an audience to your attention seekers.
✓ Over time, they become a kind of non-verbal 'shorthand' that you use to 'talk' to your class.

Your entire body plays a part in communicating with your students – from the face right down to the feet. Below you'll find advice about the effective use of different parts of your body:

The eyes and eyebrows
The eyes are 'the window to the soul', so use them to build relationships with your students and to manage their behaviour.

✓ When you're addressing a class, keep your eyes moving around, checking that all the faces are staring back at you.
✓ If they're not, pause. Don't continue talking until you have everyone's attention.

✓ Scan around the classroom while activities are taking place: nip any misbehaviour in the bud.
✓ Use your 'deadly stare' with older students – a quick glance/ glare that says 'don't push it'.
✓ Raise your eyebrows to express surprise or disapproval.
✓ If you're able, raise a single eyebrow to say: 'Excuse me, exactly what do you think you are doing?'

Your students will quickly get used to seeing you use your eyes to give non-verbal signals. When a class is not paying attention, try taking away eye contact from the class and looking instead at the ceiling. Where the teacher normally makes constant eye contact, this removal clearly indicates 'I'm waiting'.

The face

Your students spend a fair amount of time looking at your face. If they see it is constantly moving, smiling and relaxed, but always alert, then they will believe that you are in charge. Your face also betrays any tension or defensiveness you feel, so make a conscious effort to keep your expressions cool and calm.

The hands

Our hands are incredibly expressive – we 'talk' with them to our students almost as readily as we do with our voices. A teacher who uses his hands as a natural part of the teaching process engages the children and creates a feeling of inclusiveness.

Hand signals become part of your 'shorthand' with a class – you can quickly tell them what you want without needing to speak. You could:

Early years

✓ Put a finger to your lips to indicate that you want silence.
✓ Tug on your ear to show that the children must listen.

Primary

✓ Click your fingers to gain an individual's attention.
✓ Place your hand on the desk of a student who is misbehaving.

Secondary

✓ Hold one hand out, palm outwards, to say 'stop!'.
✓ Give a 'thumbs up' signal to show well done.

Further education

✓ Make a circular motion with your fingers as you elucidate a point.
✓ Hold one finger upwards in the air to say 'wait'.

The body: stance

The stance that you take with your body communicates a great deal to the class, as does your overall posture. Aim to look confident – stand tall and keep your body open and relaxed. Use different positions to indicate your wishes. For instance, stand with your arms folded when you are waiting to begin the lesson, to suggest that you will not start teaching until the class do as you wish.

The body: actions and non-actions

As the saying goes, 'actions speak louder than words': teachers should develop a whole repertoire of different actions to 'talk' to their students. You might look pointedly at your watch, to indicate that a class is wasting (their own) time. You could write down a student's name during an incident of misbehaviour (this can make them stop and check to find out what you are writing and why).

By refusing to take any action at all you send as powerful a non-verbal signal as doing something. For instance, you can call the class's bluff by waiting for silence, refusing to start work until the students cooperate. Or you might literally 'freeze' like a statue to surprise your class into listening.

The body: levels

If the teacher always stands upright, and above the students, he communicates a subtle message of superiority over them. However, although you want to be in control of the situation, this is not the same as suggesting that you are more important than your students. When you vary your body levels, you:

✓ Show your students that you are confident in your ability to keep control
✓ Show that you respect them enough to come down to their level, both literally and metaphorically
✓ Lessen any perceived sense of authority or intimidation
✓ Communicate much more effectively on a one-to-one basis
✓ Keep your interactions private.

Sitting on the floor can work well, particularly alongside very young students. Similarly, sitting or even standing on a desk creates an interesting shift in perspective.

The body: appearance

Although it is not politically correct to admit it, your students make judgements about you based on how you look. Good grooming helps, but barring cosmetic surgery, there's not an awful lot you can do about your appearance. In any case, it's not about whether you are good-looking or ugly, fat or thin, but about how you express your inner sense of self through the way you look.

Being smartly turned out makes a good impression on some older students – it suggests you take yourself and your job seriously. For some teachers looking scruffy and unconventional works well, because of the power of their personalities. Certain subjects or age groups lend themselves to creative or casual clothing: you wouldn't get down on the ground in an Armani suit to study a worm with a 3-year-old.

The teacher within the space

The way you use your teaching space communicates a complex non-verbal message about your style, and your levels of control. When we feel defensive, we might back into a corner, a place of safety. Unfortunately, unless you've used a seating plan, the rebels will be formulating their plans for revolution at the back of the classroom. And if you're stuck at the front, you won't be able to deal with them.

Teaching is a *physical* as well as an intellectual occupation, so get yourself moving around the room. Aim to:

- ✓ **Stand proud**: no matter how bad you are feeling, try not to let your body show it. Even when the class is rioting, stand up straight and proud, and give off an air of confidence.
- ✓ **Mark your territory**: move around the teaching space, whenever your energy levels allow. Do this when the students are doing an activity, but also while you are explaining the lesson. This 'marks' the space as yours.
- ✓ **Surprise them**: keep your students on their toes – make sure they never know when you will be approaching from behind.
- ✓ **Visit everyone**: be sure to 'visit' everyone during the course of each lesson. Watch for your natural tendency to move to your 'dominant' side (probably your left side if you are left-handed.)
- ✓ **Use all the space**: stand at the back, the side, in the doorway – see your room from a range of perspectives. Sit in their seats too, so you understand how you appear to your students during lessons. Watch that you don't direct more of your teaching to one side of the room than to the other (typically to your dominant side).
- ✓ **Get close to the characters**: move in close whenever you spot any trouble brewing. Your physical presence will hopefully stamp it out before it takes hold. There is normally no need to say anything – students quickly become uncomfortable about messing around with a teacher standing close by.
- ✓ **Give 'em a shock**: sometimes it is useful to suddenly change the spatial aspects of your style or your teaching space. You might rearrange the room from groups of desks to rows; clear the

desks away and ask the class to sit on the floor; or even turn all the desks round to face in the opposite direction. Rearranging your space helps the students take a fresh perspective on what will happen in the room.

Psychological aspects of teaching

Effective teaching is not just about verbal and non-verbal communication. There are also various psychological approaches that you can use to help you manage behaviour. It's as much about keeping yourself in a positive frame of mind as it is about keeping control over your class. Ideally, you should feel calm, relaxed, but alert. Below are a few suggestions to help you achieve this state of mind:

- ✓ **Keep 'em guessing**: although consistency is important for your students, it doesn't pay to be too predictable all the time. Sometimes (and do it sparingly) make a sudden change in your teaching style. Perhaps you are normally quiet and firm. Once in a while, show them that you have another, louder and sharper, side to you.
- ✓ **Turn on a penny**: sometimes you can make a sudden change in your manner if you feel it is necessary. For instance, you are having a really good lesson, when Matthew decides to spoil things by messing around. Turn to him, say, 'How dare you spoil this lesson for my wonderful class!' and then become 'sweetness and light' again.
- ✓ **Convince yourself**: if you can convince yourself, really convince yourself, that you are in charge, then you will appear to be so. If you truly know where you're coming from (are aware) and exactly what you want (are definite) then the psychological battle is practically won.
- ✓ **Maintain a psychological distance**: although it is hard, learn to keep an emotional distance from the misbehaviour that you encounter at work. Refuse to become emotionally involved with incidents of poor behaviour and this will help you retain a sense of distance and a feeling of control.

✓ **Don't take it personally**: rather than viewing poor behaviour as an attack on you, it is far more effective and meaningful to take a sympathetic view. Remind yourself that students who misbehave generally have some sort of serious problems of their own. At the end of the day, no matter how badly behaved your classes are, it really is not the end of the world, so don't allow yourself to view it in that way.

5

Teaching styles

What is a teaching style?

There are as many styles of teaching as there are teachers, because we are all individuals who work in our own unique ways. Lots of facets go together to make up a teaching style: your personality, the way you look, the way you speak, the way you use movement and space, the levels of control you use; in fact everything you do in the classroom (and beyond) adds to your own personal teaching style.

Each teacher's style is developed over the course of time. When you first start out in the classroom, you may use a style that suggests uncertainty or a lack of confidence. Unless you are hugely self-assured, this is almost inevitable. You need a chance to experiment, to make mistakes and to find your feet. It's worth remembering that you don't have to be the same person, as a teacher, that you are outside the classroom. You can put on a confident and outgoing teacher 'character', even if you feel shy and insecure inside. It is as much about student perception as it is about reality.

Whatever style you end up using, there are certain aspects and approaches that will help you best manage your students' behaviour. You can make a conscious decision to incorporate these strategies into your style, to help you control your students' behaviour. An effective teaching style lets your class know that you are in charge, but in a positive, respectful and humanitarian way.

Developing an assertive teaching style

Teaching styles fall somewhere along a line between passive, assertive and aggressive, with an assertive style being the ideal approach for effective behaviour management. It's important to understand the elements of these different approaches, so you can get as close as possible to the right balance in your own teaching. Some of us lean naturally towards an aggressive, authoritarian teaching style, and need to curb our instinctive tendency to get wound up or overreact. Others of us will tend towards a passive, defensive approach, and need to build up our confidence, self-assurance and self-belief.

Consider where you fall on the following spectrum:

Passive	Assertive	Aggressive

To understand the spectrum better, it's useful to come up with some metaphors to describe the three styles (this is as close to a 'theory' as I'm going to get in this book, so hold tight). For instance, if you were thinking about styles of music, you might be looking at:

Easy Listening	Rock	Thrash Metal

Or if you were using food as a metaphor, you could come up with:

Milk pudding	Peperami	Super-hot chilli

The conditions in which you work have an impact on the style you adopt. If you face lots of difficult behaviour, you can feel 'under attack' from the students and tend to 'fight back' by becoming equally aggressive. But the more challenging the students, the more likely they are to react badly to an overly aggressive teaching style. In an 'easy' school (if there is such a thing), you can tend towards over-passivity, allowing the students to take control. Ironically, it's in an 'easy' school that you probably need to add a bit of fire to your style.

Let's look in more detail at the three points on the spectrum.

A passive style

✓ Is characterized by inactivity – the teacher stays 'inside' herself, and is introverted and inward-looking.
✓ She uses a quiet voice and defensive postures.
✓ The students control the classroom, rather than the teacher.
✓ The teacher uses more questions than statements.
✓ The students are unsure what the teacher wants.

Here's an example from a classroom with a passive teacher:

> *Rina is holding a paper aeroplane. She's disrupting the lesson by threatening to throw it across the room.*

Teacher:	Rina, what are you doing with that?
Rina:	Nothing.
Teacher:	Are you sure you're not doing anything?
Rina:	Of course I'm sure. [*She throws the plane. The rest of the students start making their own planes.*]
Teacher:	But you said you weren't doing anything!

An aggressive style

✓ The teacher tends to come 'out' of herself and 'at' the students.
✓ She will often overreact to what is a relatively minor misbehaviour.

✓ There are clearly defined standards, but these are often overly stringent.
✓ The teacher offers little or no flexibility when handling behaviour.
✓ Her body language is hostile and she has a tendency to shout a lot.
✓ There is the potential for serious 'blow-ups' if a student decides to take this teacher on.

Here's an example from a classroom with an aggressive teacher:

Rina is holding a paper aeroplane. She's disrupting the lesson by threatening to throw it across the room.

Teacher:	[*shouting*] What on earth do you think you're doing? Give me that right now!
Rina:	But Miss, I was only . . .
Teacher:	Don't give me that rubbish. Are you stupid or something? Aeroplane. Give it to me. Now.
Rina:	Don't shout at me.
Teacher:	Don't tell me what to do.
Rina:	I'm not staying in your stupid lesson.
Teacher:	How dare you call my lesson stupid!
Rina:	I'm out of here. [*She storms out.*]
Teacher:	Where the hell do you think you're going?! You're in serious trouble now . . .

An assertive style

✓ The teacher asserts her control of the situation.
✓ At the same time, she remains reasonable and polite with her requests.
✓ She has clear, consistent and realistic expectations about behaviour and learning.
✓ She is sure that her students can live up to these expectations.
✓ She is flexible when the situation merits.
✓ The teacher's body language and voice usage are relaxed yet confident.

✓ She stays calm and polite at all times, treating the students as she wishes to be treated.

Here's an example from a classroom with an assertive teacher:

Rina is holding a paper aeroplane. She's disrupting the lesson by threatening to throw it across the room.

Teacher:	Rina, give me that paper aeroplane right now, please.
Rina:	No.
Teacher:	Rina, I want you to give me the paper aeroplane right now.
Rina:	But it's mine.
Teacher:	Rina, if you continue to argue you will force me to put you in detention. [*Holds out hand and speaks very firmly.*] Give the paper aeroplane to me *now*.

Rina hands the paper aeroplane to the teacher.

Achieving an assertive style

In the day-to-day realities of your work, your style will bob around on the spectrum between the different points. This is partly to do with your personality, but it is also to do with how you as a human being feel on a particular day. In addition, you'll be responding to the class, or to individuals within it. The more consistent a style you can achieve, the more secure your students will feel. With experience you learn how to achieve a consistently assertive style. In the meantime, a great rule of thumb is: 'Ask once nicely, then once firmly, then get on with it.'

Effective teaching styles

You know yourself what kind of teaching style you must use, because at its base it is a product of your personality. There's no point trying to copy those strict teachers at your school if you're petite, have a quiet voice and hate conflict. When we first start out in teaching, our style is often a pretty direct copy of our normal personality. With experience, we hone our style so that we present those aspects of ourselves that are going to work best in the classroom. We might temper our natural tendency to get overexcited, or work on our normal inclination to talk really slowly.

The style you use also needs to vary according to the age of the students you work with, and the kind of environment you're teaching in. Have a look at the list below, and see whether any of these phrases seem to describe your style:

- Strict and scary
- Firm but fair
- Comic and quirky
  (I look at these three commonly chosen styles in detail below)
- Earth mother
- Brisk and business-like
- Engaging eccentric
- Drama queen
- One of the lads
- One of the kids
- Edge of madness
  (This last one is my own preferred style: the students never know quite where you're coming from, or what you're going to do next.)

Some teachers refine their style to perfection – their reputation as this 'type' of teacher is known around the school. (As in 'Watch out for Mrs Davies, she's really strict and scary'.) You might end up with a hotchpotch of bits of various different styles (particularly if you teach very varied age groups or subjects). In a secondary school you might be a bit 'strict and scary' with your Year 7 form group, and more 'one of the lads' when you teach Year 11 PE.

The 'strict and scary' teacher

Most of us know a strict and scary teacher: maybe you work with one; perhaps you were taught by one when you were at school; maybe you use aspects of this style yourself with some classes. The strict and scary teacher:

- Demands perfect behaviour at all times
- Has a high level of control over the students
- Loves to line a class up
- Feels that working in complete silence is great
- Sets the rules with no room for negotiation
- Will often shout when applying a sanction
- Uses more sanctions than rewards.

Advantages:

✓ The students learn that they must behave, or they will be punished. It becomes progressively easier to discipline them, once they understand the tight boundaries.
✓ The class is well disciplined, and a good deal of work takes place.
✓ Well-behaved students are not disrupted by their less well-behaved counterparts.
✓ The teacher does not have to strive to be in a good, fun mood all the time.
✓ She can relieve some of her stress by shouting at the class!

Disadvantages:

✗ This style is physically tiring for the teacher.
✗ If there's a lot of shouting, the teacher's voice may suffer.
✗ The teacher needs to be physically imposing for this style to work, or to have a strong 'presence'.
✗ Some of the quieter students can end up in a state of fear.
✗ There is less opportunity for explorative, creative, or group work, because the teacher needs to maintain silence for the style to be consistent.
✗ Although the students behave for this type of teacher, they are unlikely to actually like her.
✗ There is more potential for serious confrontations.

The 'firm but fair' teacher

The students like the firm but fair teacher and at the same time respect her. Many teachers aspire to this style: it is the 'ideal' one in many situations. The firm but fair teacher:

- Tells the students about the behaviour she expects
- Sticks to her rules consistently
- Applies some flexibility where it seems appropriate
- Raises her voice if needed, but only on rare occasions
- Uses interesting activities and sets hard but achievable targets
- Focuses on positive methods of motivation
- Uses more rewards than sanctions
- Gets to know her students as individuals.

Advantages:

✓ The students learn to behave through the application of consistent boundaries.
✓ Once they understand where the boundaries are, they follow them without having to be told.
✓ The class is well disciplined, and a good amount of learning takes place.
✓ This style is more relaxed, and less stressful for both teacher and students.
✓ There is less chance of confrontations arising.
✓ There is more opportunity for creative, exploratory learning.

Disadvantages:

✗ There's a fine balance to achieve between being 'fair' and becoming overly 'relaxed'.
✗ The teacher must be relentlessly consistent in applying the boundaries.
✗ This is tough when you're tired, stressed or overworked.
✗ The teacher needs to be in a good mood all of the time.
✗ Some less well-behaved students may take advantage.
✗ The style/teacher can end up being a bit dull.

The 'comic and quirky' teacher

This is the style you often see in films about teaching. It's the fun, inspirational, slightly eccentric teacher that I hope you too had when you were at school. Although firm but fair is ideal, what's missing is that little bit of spice which makes the students and the lessons come to life. The comic and quirky teacher:

- Makes her lessons fun and interesting.
- Tries to get the students to forget about misbehaving because they're having too much fun.
- Is keen for students to love learning and love her lessons.
- Is good at being flexible when needed.
- Is not so good at being consistent, because she's not convinced that it's more important than good relationships.
- Uses lots of tone and is not afraid to make a fool of herself.
- Has a tendency to stand on furniture.
- Is popular with her students.

Advantages:

✓ The students have fun – a very underrated quality in education.
✓ They often 'forget' to misbehave.
✓ Learning takes precedence over management/control.
✓ This style is very relaxed; there's very little stress for the teacher.
✓ There is little chance of confrontation.
✓ There is loads of opportunity for exploratory learning, with lots of creative thinking going on.

Disadvantages:

✗ Is not so popular with the management.
✗ There's a balance to achieve between being 'fun' and 'relaxed'.
✗ Some of her experiments will go wrong.
✗ The class will often be one of the noisiest.
✗ Some quieter students can feel overwhelmed by this style.
✗ This teacher isn't always great at dealing with quiet individuals.
✗ Some students don't respond well to a humorous style, and might take some of the teacher's jokes in the wrong way.

Enhancing your teaching style

You can incorporate many subtle variations into your teaching style. Experiment with different approaches to see what works best for your students and for you. Here are some suggestions for refining and enhancing your teaching style.

Buck the trend

Students are quick to stereotype the kind of style they expect from you, depending on the way you look. If you're a physically imposing, rugby-playing kind of bloke, they probably expect a 'strict and scary' approach. Buck the stereotype and challenge their perceptions by using a counter-intuitive approach.

Be a real person

It's a tricky balance between being a teacher and giving the students the sense that you are actually a human being as well. Being self-deprecating works very well in achieving the 'real person' effect. When you make a mistake, be willing to admit it. Be brave enough to laugh at yourself if you say something stupid. Don't be afraid to make a fool of yourself.

Don't try and be friends

Many new teachers make the mistake of getting friendly with their students, in the hope of keeping them on side. This is particularly tempting if you are close in age to them. Remember, though, doing this makes it hard to crack down on any boundary testing. Stay one step removed from your students, no matter how well you get on with them.

Retain a 'mystique'

Although you want your students to see you as a real person, it is not a good idea to give too much of yourself away. Teaching is not your entire life: it's psychologically beneficial to keep part of yourself separate from your work. Make it plain that you have a full and interesting private life, but one that you wish to keep private. Let slip brief hints if you like, but if you've got a Facebook page, make sure your students don't find it.

Create a reputation

It's really rewarding to overhear students talking positively about your lessons with their peers. Word of mouth about a teacher has a huge impact on student behaviour (for good or for bad!). Remember, our students discuss us outside of class, just as we discuss them. To build a good reputation you might:

- ✓ **Stay in the same place for a while**: as time goes by, your reputation (good, I hope) precedes you. Often you'll come across younger brothers and sisters of those students you've already taught. And I assure you, they've been discussing you at home before they arrive.
- ✓ **Use an unusual activity or lesson**: an inspiring activity influences your students' behaviour; it also helps you earn a good reputation. See Chapter 7 on p. 101 for some examples of unusual starters or activities.
- ✓ **Be an entertainer**: when students view you as an entertaining, fun, interesting teacher, they tell their peers about you. When these students come to you, at some future point, they already have positive expectations.
- ✓ **Get involved**: if your personal circumstances allow, put in some time beyond your working day. Get involved with extra-curricular activities, go along to support a sports team, help out with fundraising events. When the students see you committing yourself to them beyond what you must, this creates the sense that you care about them.

Maintaining a positive approach

Teaching is not just about dealing with poorly behaved students; it is also about working with all those wonderfully well-behaved students as well. Too much focus on dealing with difficult students can really slant your perspective, and also damage your prospects when it comes to managing everyone's behaviour. Aim to focus on the well-behaved students, getting the critical mass on your side. These students might even influence the behaviour of the few remaining troublemakers, who start to feel like the odd ones out.

With a positive approach, you retain your sense of humour and perspective, and you are far less likely to get stressed when things go wrong. You have a choice: see everything that happens in a positive light, or let it make you cynical and bad tempered. If you work with very challenging students, I appreciate that it's easy to slip into a negative approach. When your students are ignoring you, being defiant, shouting abuse, it is all too tempting to expect the worst. The tension builds up inside you, even before the lesson begins. But remember, it's never every single student in a group behaving badly, no matter how much it feels like it. To maintain a positive outlook:

✓ **Focus on what's going well**: sometimes the best way to deal with a difficult individual is to totally ignore that student. Providing the behaviour is not affecting the learning for the rest of the class, don't pay it any attention. Give yourself permission to focus on the well-behaved students for a while. Show that good behaviour is the way to get your attention.

✓ **Focus on your achievements**: take a moment to consider all the things that you are achieving. Perhaps getting the students to stay in their seats, or to listen when you want to address the class, actually represents a huge achievement.

✓ **Keep yourself fresh**: teaching is exhausting, especially at those times of year when there are lots of meetings, parents' evenings and other demands outside of school hours. Leave yourself time for a life outside school – this will help you keep your style fresh and positive.

✓ **Don't get defensive**: it's easy to slip into a frame of mind where you see everything in the worst possible light. React from your head and not from your heart, refusing to allow incidents of misbehaviour to cloud your whole style.

✓ **Use positive language**: make a simple change in the type of language you use to achieve a more positive atmosphere in your lessons. Greet your students by saying, 'Great to see you! I'm really looking forward to the brilliant work you're going to do today!' With such a positive approach, even the most cynical or jaded will be tempted to live up to your expectations.

6

Using rewards and sanctions

Why use rewards and sanctions?

In life, we get rewarded when we do well, and sanctioned when we break the rules. With some rewards and sanctions it's clear-cut: you turn up to work every day at least partly for the tangible reward of a salary; if you break the speed limit in your car and get caught, you get a fine and points on your driving licence. With other rewards and sanctions the situation is far more subtle: perhaps your biggest reward for being a teacher is the chance to 'make a difference'; maybe you stick to the speed limit near schools because you feel it's right to do.

Since I first wrote this book, I've come to understand that the whole area of rewards and sanctions is far more subtle and complex than I had assumed. I've even read books which suggest that rewards are actually damaging to our relationship with our students. However, I think most teachers would still agree that rewards and sanctions are a very useful strategy in the whole toolbox of potential techniques. Certainly, they are used in pretty much every setting I've ever visited.

Rewards are helpful because:

- ✓ They help us encourage good behaviour and hard work.
- ✓ They help us motivate our students, particularly those who do not have a natural inclination to try hard.
- ✓ They encourage us to take positive approaches with our students.
- ✓ They can boost students who have low self-esteem.

Remember: a reward doesn't have to be a material 'thing'. The best reward of all is a smile, a kind word, knowing you've pleased someone.

Sanctions are helpful because:

✓ They give us a way of getting our students to stick within the boundaries we have set.
✓ They clarify the rules – if you do A, the reward is B; if you do X, the sanction is Y.
✓ They help teach students about social mores – those written and unwritten rules and moral codes that sustain our society.

Remember: a sanction that works really well in one setting, or with a particular age group, might be no use at all with another.

Some thoughts on rewards

We all respond better to the carrot rather than the stick – to being encouraged towards something good, rather than being pushed away from something bad. When you're using rewards and sanctions aim for a ratio of about 5 to 1 in favour of rewards. Think about what motivates your particular students, and how you can capitalize on it. Look at the class both as a group and as a set of individuals. For the whole group, you can use rewards that work via peer pressure. With individuals, you can differentiate the rewards you use to suit the particular student.

Rewards and your students

Some students would work hard and behave even if you didn't give them specific rewards – they have 'intrinsic-' or self-motivation. These students can defer gratification – they will suffer short-term pain (slogging through the 'boring bits'), because they understand the long-term benefits of a good education. This could be because they:

- Are naturally well motivated

- Have an instinctive curiosity, and are fascinated by learning
- Have been taught that education is valuable
- Enjoy working hard and doing well
- Find learning easy
- Have a family that pushes them to achieve
- Want to be successful to escape a background of deprivation.

Other students lack an inner drive and can't keep themselves motivated. These students need a diet of rewards and reassurance – lots of extrinsic rewards, such as stickers, certificates, phone calls home, etc. Effectively, you are replicating the characteristics listed above for these students who don't have them. You might:

✓ Drop in regular rewards, to encourage them to reach targets
✓ Contact their family, to explain how to support the student
✓ Be a positive role model, someone who expects them to achieve great things
✓ Make the learning rewarding, to build motivation
✓ Differentiate learning to make it accessible
✓ Show them the connection between education and work.

Getting rewards to work

To make rewards work for you, adapt them to suit your situation. Although your school or college will have a policy on using rewards, you can also get creative with your approaches. (With sanctions, consistency of use and application is much more important.) Some of the most useful rewards run close to the wind – decide how far you can or should go. This depends on your own values and opinions, and also on what your school allows. For instance, to keep a difficult class focused, you might offer them a highly valued reward of their choice (listening to music, eating chocolate). Although this is not strictly allowed, sometimes it's a case of 'whatever works'.

When you're using rewards, these tips will get you the best results:

✓ **Rewards must be wanted**: it's pointless to use rewards your students don't want. For a reward to have meaning, it must be valued by the recipient – they must want to receive it. Sometimes, teachers are not helped by the rewards in their school behaviour policy, which don't really fit the students.

✓ **Don't bribe them, surprise them**: studies have shown that the most effective reward is one received unexpectedly. Rather than telling your students 'if you do this you get this', a surprise reward is given out of the blue for some pleasing work or behaviour.

✓ **Make rewards age specific**: different rewards work best with different age groups. Typically, the older the students, the more they want rewards which have monetary value (CD vouchers, stationery). Sometimes, the opposite effect occurs, where a group of 15-year-olds loves getting stickers.

✓ **Make them earn the rewards**: ensure that students earn their rewards fully, rather than handing them out for any old bit of good behaviour or work. The harder they are to get, the more they are valued. Where rewards are overused by some teachers, this devalues the currency for the rest of the staff.

✓ **Fit the reward to the individual**: within a class, there will be some who are desperate to get stickers, others for whom a phone call home is the ultimate prize. Be specific with your rewards – tailor them to the individual as far as you can.

✓ **Rewards have a sell-by date**: a reward might work well at first, then gradually run out of steam as the students get used to receiving it. Regularly refresh the rewards system you use – both as an individual teacher and as a setting.

✓ **Reward all your students**: sometimes you'll feel yourself getting trapped into giving lots of rewards to your tricky students, to keep them on your side and to get them to cooperate. But don't overlook those who work hard all the time – they deserve to receive recognition for their efforts as well.

✓ **Sometimes rewards need to be private**: most of the time, rewards are given publicly. Some students, however, won't want others to witness their success – the peer group pressure against good work or behaviour is too great. If this is the situation in which you teach, share your positive thoughts in private.

Types of rewards

Reward systems tend to be very similar in different kinds of educational establishments. Typically stickers, merits, certificates and home/school contacts prevail. Some schools are becoming more innovative with the rewards that they offer, and you will find some of these more unusual ideas below. At post-16 level, it's tricky to find meaningful material rewards. Of course the most valuable reward is free and easy to give – praise from a teacher who the students respect and like (it's earning that respect in the first place that's the hard part).

Below are some thoughts about rewards that you can use with your students. Most of these are applicable to pretty much any age group (I've suggested some adaptations as appropriate).

Individual rewards

✓ **Merits/commendations**: with well-motivated students, merit systems often work well. A useful 'add-on' to a merit system is to give the students points for their merits. They can 'cash in' points for vouchers, etc.

✓ **Certificates**: many schools use some kind of certificate to reward good behaviour or work, and these are often presented at a whole-school assembly. Adapt this idea in creative ways – 'student of the week', 'friend of the week', the class votes for a winner, and so on.

✓ **'Special' tasks**: students love being offered 'adult' tasks, and at the same time this is useful for the teacher. Tidying resources, handing out books, that kind of thing. Try 'you be teacher', where the student gets to teach the class for a few minutes.

✓ **Stickers**: in schools where I've worked, these have been effective from nursery right up to GCSE level and beyond. (At 16+ years, they become a joke between student and teacher.) You can get personalized stickers that include your name or subject. Think ahead about where you want students to put their stickers: on a jumper, a shoe, an exercise book, I even had one student who would put them on his face!

✓ **Phone calls home**: teachers tend to use phone calls home as a punishment for poor behaviour, but they are actually very effective as a reward. Catch a difficult student on a good day, promise a phone call home if he behaves well, and start to build a more positive relationship. Before phoning, check first about your school system for home/school contacts.

✓ **Writing home:** at the start of the year, hand every student a postcard and ask them to address these with their home address. Pop the pile in your drawer, and aim to fill out three or so each lesson. The great thing about a postcard, as opposed to a standardized letter, is that it can be stuck with a magnet on a fridge door, as a constant reminder of the teacher's approval.

✓ **Sweets and other treats:** when I first started teaching, no one would have raised an eyebrow if you gave out some sweets to your students. These days, with the 'healthy eating agenda', it's a brave teacher who tries this approach. Suffice to say, these do prove a popular motivator. My advice? If you do decide to hand out chocolate, get your students to eat up in class.

✓ **Raffles:** the teacher gives out raffle tickets for good work or behaviour, and then holds a draw at the end of the lesson or the week, with a prize given to the winner. Sometimes these raffles are held across the school, and for longer periods of time (e.g. a term), with really good prizes at the end.

Group rewards

Group rewards work well, because they utilize peer-group pressure. Push your students into working together to achieve these rewards.

✓ **'Special' time:** the chance to earn privileges is a very effective reward – it shows the link between good behaviour and positive consequences. The idea of a special (golden) time is widely used in primary classrooms: the students earn (or lose) the right to free-choice time on a Friday. Adapt for older students with 5 minutes' 'social time' at the end of lessons.

✓ **Music:** earning the 'right' to listen to music is popular with older students, although using it clearly depends on the subject being taught. Use a radio, rather than allowing students to bring in their own music (or you may get issues with inappropriate language).

✓ **Marbles in a jar**: the teacher has an empty jar on his desk; every time a student works hard or behaves well, a marble goes in the jar. When the jar is full, the class receives a treat (for instance a picnic with takeaway pizza).
✓ **Trips**: the chance to go on a trip is a powerful motivator. It has the added benefit of leaving a very positive and beneficial 'afterglow' for those involved, and of course it's educationally valuable too. One drawback is that it requires a lot of work to organize this kind of event.

For more rewards you might use, visit www.suecowley.co.uk, where you'll find a free downloadable document listing loads of different ideas.

Some thoughts on sanctions

No one likes to be punished: giving a sanction has the potential to do damage to your relationships with your students. So, when you do have to use sanctions, you've got to get it right. Consider your own response to the threat of being punished. You're driving along the road when you see a speed camera. What happens when you reach those white lines on the road (I'm assuming you slow down)? And what makes you behave in that way? For the sanction to work, you need to be:

✓ Aware of what the rules are in the first place
✓ Aware of what the punishment is for breaking them
✓ Fairly certain you will get caught if you break the rules
✓ Sure that if you are caught, you will get punished
✓ Worried enough about the punishment to want to avoid getting it.

Exactly the same principles apply when you use sanctions with your students. If they know what the rules are, and they don't want the sanction they'll get for breaking them, you are halfway there.

The best approach to using sanctions is to stick closely to your behaviour policy: consistent use of sanctions is best for staff and fairest for students. A great tip is to 'blame the policy' – your role when giving sanctions is one of enforcer – you are applying the rules set by the organization. Your main job is to teach, not to discipline. Sometimes your policy does not serve you or your students well, or does not include sanctions that the students wish to avoid. If that's the case, you'll need to duck and dive a bit to get things right. To make the most effective use of sanctions:

✓ **Ensure that they're unwanted**: just as rewards must be wanted, so sanctions must be something the students want to avoid. Otherwise, they won't act as an effective deterrent. If your students don't care about getting detentions, then there is little point in giving them.

✓ **Make sure they're proportionate**: if a teacher reacts to a minor offence by immediately throwing the student out of class, this suggests that he's been looking for an excuse to get rid of that person. Unless the misbehaviour is really serious, start with the lowest level sanction.

✓ **Make them fit the 'crime'**: the best sanctions give both student and teacher a sense that justice is being served. If a student scribbles on a desk, the most fitting punishment would be to clean the desks off.

✓ **Sanctions must be followed through**: when you give a sanction, it must be served, or it's pointless giving it in the first place. If it's not, next time round your students know that yours are empty threats. (With short detentions, this can mean chasing a student endlessly to serve their time – it's a lot of hassle, but it really is worth doing.)

✓ **Don't threaten what you can't or won't deliver**: when we are stressed, it is tempting to throw out threats about all the terrible things that will happen to the class if they don't stop messing around. Don't threaten something you have no intention of doing – it makes you look unreliable.

✓ **Avoid the threat of 'somebody else'**: sometimes a teacher threatens to send a student to 'somebody else' (typically a senior manager of some kind). Unfortunately, all this does is suggest that you cannot deal with the situation yourself. As a first step, aim to deal with behaviour problems yourself, only referring a student to someone else if the issue really merits it.

Types of sanctions

There are many different sanctions you can use to help you control behaviour. Remember that the most effective sanction is often the simplest – a disappointed look or a word about how unhappy you are – *provided the students respect the teacher or want to please him in the first place*. (Of course in some very challenging settings the weight of difficult behaviour means that these low-level approaches have little impact.) Unless the behaviour is very serious, start with the most minimal form of intervention, and work up gradually.

Low level
A disapproving look
A comment – 'I'm disappointed to see you do that'
A verbal warning
A sad face or name on the board
Moving towards the student
Placing a hand on the desk
A slightly raised voice, or a cross tone

Medium level
A written warning
Loss of privileges
A short break-time detention
A 'yellow card'
A 'behaviour slip' to go to a tutor or senior teacher
Being put 'on report'
A 'time-out'

> *High level*
> A 'red card'
> Getting the student removed from the lesson
> A longer after-school detention
> Speaking to parents – writing or phoning home
> Suspension or exclusion

Something else worth trying is the 'comedy sanction', especially if you have a good, jokey relationship with a class. For instance, you might threaten to sing to them if they don't stop talking (assuming your singing voice is as awful as mine!).

Some thoughts on detentions

In most secondary (and some primary) schools, detentions are one of the most frequently used sanctions, so it's vital to get them right. Depending on your school situation, detentions may work very well, or they may be of practically no use at all. You certainly need to use your professional judgement to decide whether detentions are a useful sanction. Where you do use them:

✓ **Make sure they're served**: in a secondary school, chasing students to serve detentions is often very time-consuming – that brief moment of poor behaviour in class turns into a cat-and-mouse game of epic proportions. But if you chase the first few times, the students soon realize that they might as well turn up. If you're not willing to chase up on missed detentions, you would be better off not using them at all.

✓ **Get them served asap**: ideally, there should be a clear link between the misbehaviour and the punishment, so get detentions served as quickly as possible. It is far better for students to serve an initial short detention, than for you to have to refer them for more serious sanctions.

✓ **Use a 'collection service'**: in secondary schools, a major issue is when you need a student or group to return to you at a break time or at the end of the day. If they fail to turn up, you must then chase them to serve the sanction. To avoid this, send a reliable student to go and fetch your detainee a few minutes before the bell goes (agree this with their teacher beforehand).

✓ **Think about what happens during detentions:** you might take the opportunity to have a chat about why the misbehaviour happened, and what can be done to stop it happening again. You could devise a community sanction: collecting plates in the dining hall, or picking up rubbish. If the sanction is for work not done in class time, the student should finish it in detention.

Teachers often ask me about my opinion of whole-class detentions. While I can see the arguments against (particularly that they're unfair on the well-behaved majority), I can also see that sometimes these are a necessary evil with a very chatty class. My best advice is to use them sparingly, and to try and give the class a chance to 'win back'. For instance, if the students earn a 3-minute detention because they're so chatty, they could work in silence for 3 minutes to earn back the time. When you let the students leave the whole-class detention, make sure that you send the best behaved away first.

How to apply sanctions

When you come to apply sanctions, the way that you do this has an impact on how your students react to being punished. Unless the situation is very serious, avoid confrontation by giving a series of warnings first. With very young children, a distraction is often far more effective than a sanction. This can work well with older students as well, particularly with those who are trapped in habitual misbehaviour, and who need you to show them a way out of it.

The advice below covers both the behaviour management techniques you should use when giving sanctions, and also some tips about your use of voice, body and space:

Behaviour management techniques

✓ **Defer if necessary**: don't feel that you always have to give a sanction immediately after the misbehaviour occurs. If you're trying to introduce the lesson and one child is being disruptive, you might say 'I'll talk to you about your behaviour in a moment', then go on to complete your introduction. Once the class is on task, you can then deal with the student in relative privacy. A good rule of thumb is: 'is this misbehaviour immediately interfering with my ability to teach the class?' If not, you can defer.

✓ **Make the situation clear**: misunderstandings can lead to unnecessary confrontations, so always make your position crystal clear. State your expectations clearly, telling the student exactly what you want, then clarify how the student's behaviour is failing to meet your expectations.

✓ **Make your feelings clear**: students who misbehave often have issues with a lack of empathy. Explain how the behaviour makes you and the other students feel, and how it impacts on the learning for the class. Encourage students to see how others view their behaviour, and consequently why it is unacceptable.

✓ **Offer a positive alternative**: sometimes, students back themselves into a corner when they misbehave, and it is up to you to offer them a way out. Offer a volunteer task to complete, or suggest an alternative activity.

✓ **Sanction the behaviour, not the student**: the problem is not the student, but the student's behaviour. Remember this to help you keep sanctions depersonalized. 'When you talk over me, the class can't hear what I'm saying' as opposed to 'Sam, you're talking again, why are you always talking?' Your use of sanctions is not a personal attack on the student, but a logical and consistent response to the student's behaviour.

✓ **Use 'the choice'**: this strategy, described in Chapter 3, helps you depersonalize sanctions, and throws the responsibility for the situation back on the student. The choice is simple: 'Either you stop the behaviour now, or you will force me to apply this particular sanction.' Don't feel guilty if the student pushes you into giving a punishment.

Use of voice, body and space

✓ **Keep it private**: move beside the student, or ask him to step outside for a moment to talk with you. Use a quiet voice, so that the rest of the class can't hear. If you embarrass the student in front of his peers, this ups the stakes and can lead to confrontation. Don't give your troublemakers the 'oxygen of publicity'.

✓ **Remember! Repetition is vital**: repeat a warning to ensure it's been heard. Say the student's name several times to make sure he is listening. Don't assume something will be heard the first time you say it.

✓ **Tell, don't ask**: assert yourself by the use of positive commands, rather than using questions which suggest the behaviour is optional. Use 'I want' and 'I need you to' statements, rather than 'Could you' or 'Will you'. Tell your students exactly what you want them to do – they need to know.

✓ **Stay relaxed**: keep your responses calm and casual. Before you speak, breathe deeply a few times to ensure you are rational rather than emotional. If possible, coax the student into complying, rather than wading straight in with a sanction.

✓ **Be polite**: if a student is rude and defiant, you may feel tempted to blow off steam by being rude yourself. Don't descend to the same level – remember, model the behaviour you want to see.

✓ **Use a tone of regret, rather than revenge**: aim to sound unhappy and disappointed that the student has forced you to use a sanction.

Of course, when you sanction you won't always be dealing with an individual – sometimes several students will be misbehaving simultaneously. When this happens, you could:

✓ Deal with the worst offender first, to make an example of him.

✓ Deal with the easiest student first, and hope the others notice.

✓ Use a completely non-verbal approach – look cross, then turn to the board and start writing up names.

✓ Take a positive approach – single out some well-behaved students.

✓ Grab a pile of behaviour slips and start to fill them out.
✓ Aim to distract everyone by making a sudden change in the
  lesson.

Here are two examples of a teacher applying a sanction, showing
how the student might react to different approaches.

✓ *A good way to apply sanctions*

*Carly has arrived at her Year 9 science lesson in a very bad mood. She is
wandering around the room, chatting to the other students. The teacher is
ready to take the register and wants to start the lesson.*

Teacher: Carly, I need to get going with my lesson now. Could
              you hand out these exercise books for me while I take
              the register?
Carly: [*distracted by this*] Oh, okay.

*Later in the lesson Carly gets up again and starts to wander around. The
teacher motions her to one side to speak privately with her.*

Teacher: Carly. We have a rule that we stay in our seats in
              science: it's really important for everyone's safety. I
              need you to sit down right now please.
Carly: No I won't. I'm bored. This lesson is stupid.
Teacher: Well, Carly, I'm sorry that you feel that way. You have
              a choice. Sit down right now, get your work done and
              go on time. Or I'm afraid you will force me to give
              you a detention.
Carly: That's not fair! I'm not doing anything wrong!
Teacher: Carly. I want you to sit down in your seat *right now* and
              get on with your work. Last chance. Don't push it.

*At this stage Carly will either comply or the teacher will have to apply the
sanction.*

✗ *A bad way to apply sanctions*

Carly has arrived at her Year 9 science lesson in a very bad mood. She is wandering around the room, chatting to the other students. The teacher is ready to take the register and wants to start the lesson.

Teacher: [*across the room*] Carly! Can you sit down please? I want to start my lesson.

Carly: Well, I don't want to start your lesson. Your lessons are stupid.

Teacher: Don't be so rude! Look, why can't you just sit down and let me get on with taking the register?

The rest of the class are watching the confrontation with interest. Carly is now enjoying the 'publicity' of being sanctioned in front of the class.

Carly: No, I won't sit down. Are you gonna make me?

Teacher: Yes I am going to make you. You're in an hour's detention with me after the lesson.

Carly: That's not fair! I'm not coming!

Teacher: Yes you are. Now shut up and sit down.

Carly: You can't tell me to shut up! I hate you and I hate your lessons. I'm out of here!

Carly storms out of the room.

7

Teaching for good behaviour

Teaching and behaviour

In teaching, there are lots of things that you can't change or have much of an impact on. You can't change the students you have to work with; you can't change the background they come from or the local environment; you can't change the way that they've been brought up, or what their parents are like; you can't change the senior managers who run your school or college; and even though you can improve the general look of your classroom, you can't get yourself moved to a different teaching space overnight.

But the biggest thing you can change, the place where you can have the most influence, is on the way that you go about planning and teaching your lessons.

It's important to remember that the reason you need to manage behaviour in the first place is so that you can get on with teaching. That's what you're in the classroom for, after all. As part of your quest to get your students behaving, you need to plan and deliver really high-quality lessons. Although this isn't a magic formula for getting perfect behaviour, it is one part of your practice that you can adapt very easily.

Think back to when you were at school. If you were in a lesson that was:

- fast paced
- engaging
- interesting
- weird

- surprising
- disgusting
- exciting
- or funny.

. . . I bet you and your peers were more likely to behave.

Not every lesson can or should be an all-singing, all-dancing, multimedia extravaganza. There will be days when you are so tired that you can barely drag yourself into school; other times when the subject you're teaching is dry and hard to spice up. But if most of your lessons are high-quality ones, your students will be more inclined to behave themselves for you. You'll also get yourself that all-important good reputation.

Of course, there's a balance to be struck between what students view as fun activities and what is educational. After all, given the choice, many would spend all day every day playing computer games, or out on the football pitch. As their teacher you must get through the curriculum and teach them the skills they need. Inevitably, it will be difficult to make some of the material you must teach stimulating, while still covering all subject areas. On the whole, though, students forgive the occasional dull lesson from a teacher who normally teaches in an inspirational way.

Before I describe how you might 'teach for good behaviour', I'd like to deal with some of those things that could stop you being more experimental and creative. You could be worried about:

- Getting through the curriculum
- What might happen if you give your trust to your students
- The noise and mess that could be created
- Whether the students will get overexcited and go wild
- What other teachers, senior managers or inspectors will think.

Let's deal with each of those concerns in turn:

'I'm worried about getting through the curriculum'
If your students are misbehaving, you can 'get through' it all you like: they probably won't learn or remember it though. Don't be a teacher who just ticks the curriculum boxes, be a teacher who wants them to learn.

'I'm worried what might happen if I give my trust to my students'

The more often you trust them, the more likely they will be to honour that trust. My experience suggests that the more 'difficult' the students, the more likely they are to respond well to being given your trust.

'I'm worried about the noise and mess that could be created'

If the noise reflects engagement with the lesson, that's a good, not a bad, thing. And if it's mess that concerns you, you can always get them to tidy up (or do it yourself if it comes to it).

'I'm worried that my students will get overexcited and go wild'

They might do, the first time you try something experimental. But when they do, you learn the techniques needed to pull back from that situation. And next time round, it won't be so hard.

'I'm worried what other teachers, senior managers or inspectors will think'

Who are you doing this for? If the answer is 'my students', then who cares what anyone else thinks? Be brave enough to use your own professional judgement, and refuse to care what others think.

If you think back to your own schooldays, I hope that you too can remember one or more teachers who really inspired you, who filled you with a passion for learning or for a particular subject. Who perhaps even inspired you to become a teacher yourself. Being in a position to inspire the next generation is an incredible honour – our influence lives on long after we do. Although teaching with passion, energy and enthusiasm is hard work at times, it has got to be worth it when you consider the potential benefits.

Effective planning and teaching

There is great skill involved in planning and delivering high-quality lessons. Learning how to plan and teach well takes time, but eventually you get a feel for what is going to be effective. With experience you also learn how to adapt your teaching for different classes and different students, sometimes even during the lesson itself. Planning quality lessons should be relaxing and enjoyable: use your imagination, and think laterally about different ways of putting across a topic.

As a trainee or new teacher, you'll have to put lots of detail in your lesson planning. Play the game and plan as your lecturers expect you to plan – a detailed plan helps you think through your lessons in advance and gives you a sense of security. However, once you qualify and begin to experiment, you might find (as I do) that too much prescriptive planning tends to work against good-quality lessons. Having too much detail in your plan can:

- Tempt you to stick to something that isn't working
- Mean you are stuck to your desk, referring to your notes, while misbehaviour is plotted at the back of the room
- Make you become unresponsive to the mood of the class
- Mean you lose the 'feel' that is needed to pace and time a lesson.

The ability to engage, interest and excite your students depends on a whole range of different factors – the format and content of a lesson, and also the way it is delivered. Get these aspects right, and you stand a much better chance of encouraging good behaviour. (You never know, your students might even totally forget about the idea of misbehaving!)

The format of lessons

Lesson format is the 'nuts and bolts' of good planning – it means giving a clear and effective structure to class time. Generally speaking, students want to have this structure to their learning, and it's particularly important for those students with behaviour issues. Good lesson format helps you keep your students focused and on task. The strategies given below will help you format your lessons effectively.

'Mapping' the lesson

Delivering a lesson is a bit like setting out on a journey – the teacher knows what the destination is (the aims, objectives, success criteria), but the students don't yet know where you're going. When you've spent ages planning a session, it's tempting to believe that the students will somehow 'know' what it is going to be about, without any explanation. If you then launch straight into the subject, the students get confused, feel a lack of clear structure and purpose, and are more likely to start messing around.

You can let your class know where the lesson is going by doing some or all of the following:

✓ Explaining your aims
✓ Talking about your objectives
✓ Establishing the success criteria
✓ Telling them your 'WALT' – 'we are learning to'
✓ Letting them know your 'WILF' – 'what I'm looking for'
✓ Writing an outline of the format up on your whiteboard
✓ Explaining the timings of the session
✓ Getting the students to devise a set of questions they'd like answered.

Not every single lesson has to have this tight, pre-ordained format. Sometimes you'll want to take a journey without having an exact sense of where you're going to end up. You might bring in an inspirational resource, or ask the class a question, to get things going. At other times, a lesson may deviate entirely from its original intention ('destination'), because you realize pretty quickly that what you had planned just doesn't suit the students.

Tasks and activities

A lesson or session is basically made up of a series of tasks or activities. The way you format these will have a significant effect on your students' behaviour. For the best results:

✓ **Keep the tasks short and focused**: the longer you spend on any one activity, the more chance there is for the students to get bored. With lots of short, purposeful exercises, you create a strong sense of focus and pace.

✓ **Set clear targets:** be sure about what and how much you want your students to achieve, whether it's five ideas or half a page. Reward the completion of each target before you move on to the next.

✓ **Set clear time limits:** similarly, be clear about how much time is available to complete the activity. If you give the average student 20 minutes, she will use half of it chatting before she begins. If it looks like the students are finishing early or need more time, stretch or condense the actual time to suit their needs.

✓ **Keep the pace up:** using short, focused tasks creates a sense of pace and forward momentum which is useful in engaging those students with poor attention spans.

✓ **Break up longer tasks:** where you need to set longer periods of time for activities, break the time up by getting the students to stop to share ideas or to discuss what they've done so far.

✓ **Use a variety:** try a mix-and-match approach – ensure that there is plenty of variety in the tasks you do. This helps you appeal to different learning styles: aural, visual, practical.

✓ **Use must/should/could:** a useful tip is to split longer tasks up into work you must do, work you should do, and work you could do. The more able will finish all three parts; the less able students have a target for what to complete.

At the end of your lesson, talk with your students about what they have achieved and reward them for hard work. Create a sense of success, so that they are more likely to behave and work well the next time you see them. A plenary gives a good sense of completion to the lesson journey.

As well as devising activities yourself, get your students involved. In the Foundation Stage, the students spend much of the time choosing the activities they want to access (although the resources you set out have an influence on what they will learn). With older students, the teacher tends to have more say in the activities they do. Instead of always being the one holding the reins, hand over the lesson journey to your students when you can.

The content of lessons

Planning and delivering the content of a lesson should be where the fun lies. Our role is to get ideas, facts, skills and information across so that our students can learn. When you make a subject accessible this gives you a sense of achievement; it also keeps your students on task and behaving themselves. Good lesson content will include some or all of the following elements:

✓ Fun
✓ Connections with the real world
✓ Multi-sensory
✓ Topical and relevant
✓ Plenty of props and resources
✓ Big, colourful, eye-catching.

Let's deal with each of these in turn.

Fun: this involves lateral thinking. Students tend to see lessons as fun if they seem as little like work as possible: it's a bit like hiding vegetables in a pasta sauce – hide the learning behind the fun. You could try:

✓ A crime scene (see p. 114)
✓ A quiz
✓ Activities based on a TV show (*Who Wants to Be a Millionaire; I'm a Celebrity, Get Me Out of Here!*)
✓ Educational games.

Connections with the real world: those students who prove most difficult to manage, often fail to see the link between education and the real world beyond. Bring this alive for them by creating real-life scenarios in your classroom. For instance, with Foundation Stage students you could:

✓ Work as 'spies' to find clues and use different mark-making methods.
✓ Become 'builders' to make a wall with bricks, sand and water.
✓ Be circus performers to practise balancing, juggling and tumbling.

Multi-sensory: in the typical lesson, students use only a limited palette of senses – often just their sight and hearing. Find ways to incorporate activities involving as many of the senses as possible. Your students could touch objects, smell plants, taste foods. Be creative whatever the curriculum area:

- ✓ In maths, sort spices (cardamom pods, star anise) rather than blocks.
- ✓ In geography, go on a sensory walk around the local area.
- ✓ In art, make 'smelly sculptures' by adding food flavourings to playdough or clay.

Topical and relevant: show how the learning relates to current events, or to the students' interests. Demonstrate that education is a fundamental part of, and not separate from, the world beyond. For instance, you could link big sports events (the World Cup, the Olympics) to learning in:

- ✓ Numeracy/maths – scoring, trajectory, stadium capacity
- ✓ Geography – flags and anthems from around the world
- ✓ Literacy/English – poems about scoring the winning goal

Plenty of props and resources: students of all ages love getting their hands on *things*, especially things that aren't normally found in a classroom. Be creative – go for the unusual to catch their attention. Have a think – what could you do in your subject/age range with:

- ✓ A pack of cards
- ✓ A toilet seat
- ✓ A lottery ticket?

When it comes to using objects, anything that makes your students go 'urrgghhh!' will work very well – a steaming pile of horse droppings, a weird-looking bug you found in your garden.

Big, colourful, eye-catching: to catch your students' attention, have fun playing around with size and colour. You could try:

✓ Using giant, oversized objects
✓ Adding vivid colours to a presentation
✓ Drawing a giant picture with chalks on the ground outside
✓ Using a simple two-tone effect of black and white for a display.

All these approaches appeal particularly to those students who prefer visual ways of learning.

Abstract concepts – concrete activities
One of the greatest skills of the practitioner or teacher is to put across tricky, abstract ideas in such a way that the students can understand them. We take an abstract concept (numbers, forces, metaphor, population spread) and find a real-life, concrete, meaningful way to make this idea come to life for our students.

A key cause of misbehaviour is when the students can't access the work. They get frustrated or embarrassed at not understanding, and they mess around to hide this. By creating concrete activities, where the students do and then understand, you make the learning far more accessible for your class.

The younger your students, the further back and more concrete you have to make the activities you use. With very young children you take the concepts right back to their most basic form. Let's look at three concepts from different age ranges and subjects, which you might want to put across to your students.

Foundation Stage
Abstract concept – that writing (letters and numbers) can be used to convey meaning.
Practical activity: the practitioner sets up a 'shop' area in her role-play corner, and puts sticky notes, clipboards and pens here. She talks with the children about how they might 'write' some 'price tickets' to go on the different items.

Primary science
Abstract concept – push, pull and forces (Newton's Third Law).
Practical activity: the teacher offers the students a range of different wheeled resources – a skateboard, a toy car, a buggy,

and some other items, such as a fan, a magnet and a rope. She challenges the students to find as many different ways to move the objects as they can.

Secondary history
Abstract concept – eyewitness accounts are often unreliable.

The teacher arranges ahead of time for a helper. She begins her lesson by talking with her students about why eyewitness accounts might be unreliable. Suddenly, her helper bursts into the room, runs up to the teacher, gives her a (pretend) smack across the face and then runs out again. The teacher asks the class to write an eyewitness account – what did they just see, what did the person look like, what was she wearing, and so on.

Where possible, add other elements to your concrete activities – make them multi-sensory, colourful, eye-catching, topical. The more of these techniques you get in place, the more likely your students are to be fully engaged with their learning.

The delivery of lessons

Effective lesson delivery is as much about teacher style and personality as it is about good planning. Use the strategies given in Chapters 4 and 5 about communication and teaching styles to help you teach in a way that encourages good behaviour. Aim to communicate:

- ✓ A sense of passion for the subject, the topic or the skill being learnt
- ✓ A love of the process of learning
- ✓ A sense of curiosity about and interest in the world
- ✓ The feeling that you are really interested in the students and you want them to be successful
- ✓ The feeling that your job in education *really matters* to you.

The amount of energy and enthusiasm you put into your work will have a direct impact on how your students feel about being with you. Some days it's hard to find the energy but it's worth it when you can.

The importance of time management

The way you control time can have a surprisingly powerful effect on behaviour, either positive or negative. Follow the dos and don'ts below to get this area of your practice just right.

Do:

✓ Take a calm, measured approach.
✓ Give each activity a suitable amount of time – not too long or too short.
✓ Be flexible about how much you can achieve: adapt to the reality of the situation.
✓ Remember, you'll have to spend some time giving rewards and possibly sanctions too.
✓ Take care over the start of lessons or sessions – use a whole-group focus to pull the class together, especially after a break.
✓ Remember, some classes respond well to a 'quick start', others need to be eased in, perhaps by taking a register.
✓ Consider the end of lessons too. Spend some time on a review, or on calming down your students if it's been a very exciting session.
✓ Aim to finish early – it's far better to eke out the last bit of a lesson than to have to rush after the session time is over.

Don't:

✗ Allow your sessions to feel rushed – you'll stress your students and they'll be more likely to misbehave.
✗ Plan to do too much during a lesson – you'll end up rushing to fit everything in.
✗ Be in a rush to get started or finished.
✗ Finish late, and have to rush everyone out or clear away yourself.
✗ Send the students away with their last impression being that of a stressed-out teacher.

A very useful activity for finishing off a session in the right frame of mind is 'statues'. I've used this activity with all ages: from early years right through to adults. Ask the students to get themselves comfy, and then say 'freeze'. They must now stay completely still for a couple of minutes (or however long is appropriate). On your signal the students 'unfreeze' and get ready to go. In primary or secondary school, get them to push their chairs behind the desks, as quietly as possible. Do this in slow motion if you like, to add a fun element.

Guaranteed to succeed

Sometimes you will just not be up to coping with a really difficult class. On these occasions you need activities and lessons that are pretty much guaranteed to encourage good behaviour. Don't feel guilty about needing the occasional lesson off from coping with misbehaviour. You're only human, and no one can work at full steam all the time. Teaching is, in many ways, like acting: you're presenting yourself to a large (and often difficult) audience. Nobody would realistically expect an actor to perform all day every day – the same applies to the exhausted teacher.

The suggestions below for lessons are practically guaranteed to succeed, even with the most difficult students/classes. They have worked for me in a variety of schools, from the 'fairly easy' to the 'downright impossible'!

- ✓ **The computer:** put a student of any age in front of a computer and you'll get, at the very least, a bit of peace and quiet. There's loads of great learning that can take place on a computer – research via the internet, creating PowerPoint slides, making a leaflet, drawing pictures.
- ✓ **DVDs:** an ex-primary-school teacher I know once told me in an interview that to get through in the toughest schools 'we watched more TV than was strictly necessary'. Even the 'class from hell' will usually sit fairly quietly to watch a video. Assuage your guilt by ensuring it's related to a subject they are studying. Make sure it's up to date and interesting enough to keep their attention.

✓ **Outside visitors**: students often respond really well to people who are not in the role of 'teacher'. It takes a bit of forward planning, but when you have a visitor it gives you a bit of a break. It's often really inspirational for your students as well. It could be a theatre group, a police officer, a parent with an exciting career, a yoga specialist, a conservation group which brings in owls for the students to handle.

As well as bringing in visitors from outside, make sure you ask around for volunteers who might be willing to support you in your setting. Many early years settings and primary schools have lots of parent volunteers helping out. The more adults in the room, the more eyes there are to watch out for any signs of misbehaviour!

Engaging activities across the curriculum

This section gives you a few ideas that I have used, or seen used, to engage a difficult (and, indeed, an easy) class. When I say 'engage', what I mean is to make the students so interested in and focused on the learning, that they forget completely about wanting to misbehave. To get your students engaged, what you're after is something that falls into one of the following categories:

✓ Bizarre
✓ Weird
✓ Surprising
✓ Unusual
✓ Strange but true
✓ Fascinating
✓ Gripping
✓ Thrilling
✓ Yucky
✓ Crazy
✓ True to life.

You're also looking for something with all those elements I discussed earlier on in this chapter – multi-sensory, topical, and so on.

The scene of the crime

Areas of learning

- Creative and lateral thinking
- Examining evidence
- Close observation
- Analysis, deduction and theorizing
- Studying texts
- The crime genre
- Mapping and drawing plans
- Forensics, samples, fair testing
- Discussion and decision-making.

Resources

- An open area (push any chairs or desks aside)
- 'Police tape' (buy the 'real thing' from my website or from www.uktapes.com)
- Props relating to the crime (a handbag with the contents spilt out, a bottle, a length of rope, money, whatever you like really)
- Plastic gloves (I save them when I fill up my car with petrol)
- 'Police report' form.

Description

I originally devised this activity to teach genre in drama: it grabs the attention of even the most difficult class. Your students should quite readily go along with the 'fiction' of the lesson. When they enter the room, tell them that there has been a crime. They must not touch anything (they will want to) – ask them why and they'll tell you all about fingerprints.

With older students your crime could be an assault or murder; with young ones, choose a gentler idea – the class toy has been taken, a pot of pencils has gone missing.

The students work as police detectives to examine the crime scene. They discuss their findings, backing up their suppositions with an analysis of the evidence (that makes it sound tricky but this can be done with students of any age, working at different levels of complexity). You can develop this activity in loads of ways, depending on the curriculum area you want to work on:

✓ Draw a detailed plan of the crime scene.
✓ Measure footprints to work out the height of the criminal.
✓ Complete a 'police report', listing evidence, identifying witnesses.
✓ Interview a suspect, recording the discussion.
✓ Do a dramatic TV reconstruction of the crime.
✓ Test forensic samples.
✓ Stage a court case, with judge, lawyers, defendant, etc.

As well as being a useful generic activity, you can also link this into specific texts. In English, I've used it to study Shakespeare's *Romeo and Juliet* by setting up the 'crime scene' from the end of the story. I've also used it to explore some of the Sherlock Holmes detective stories.

The can of dog food

Areas of learning

- Marketing and the power of persuasion (should we always believe what we read on the label?)
- Design and art skills
- What's on a label?
- Tamper-proof packaging
- Analysis of samples.

Resources

- A can of dog food or a pouch of cat food
- Chopped-up Mars bars
- Orange jelly
- A fork
- Tape or glue.

Description

This activity was originally used for design technology, and it shocks the students into paying attention. Of all the suggestions I've ever made, this has attracted the most controversy. Your teaching style probably needs to be 'comic and quirky' or possibly 'edge of madness' to pull it off. Prepare your can ahead of time: cut the base off the tin or split open the pouch carefully; empty it out and wash it well; chop up the Mars bars and mix this with the jelly; refill the can or pouch and fix it back together with glue or tape. (Note: an easier alternative is to swap the labels over between dog food and something more appetizing.)

Explain to the class that the lesson is about packaging. Show the students the can of dog food, open it up, and then eat from it. Offer it round the class, to see if anyone will have a taste. You'll get a lively reaction to this opening, but your students will eventually quieten down to hear what you have to say. You could move on to:

✓ Discuss the 'power of persuasion' and how marketing affects us.
✓ Explore what's on different labels and what it tells us.
✓ Test the contents of various cans to see what they contain.
✓ Design your own labels.

The market

Areas of learning

- Speaking and listening, building vocabulary
- Using the target language in modern foreign languages
- Money, prices, adding, subtracting
- Art, design, creative skills
- Drama characterization and improvisation
- Understanding of other cultures (foods, clothes).

Resources

- Tables to use as market stalls
- Food or other goods for the stalls

- Money (real or toy)
- Tills if you have them
- Paper and pens to create signs.

Description

This lesson was originally set in a French market place to get the students practising their language. The students set up stalls selling foods or goods. They then act as either stall-holders or visitors to the market, buying and selling goods. You can adapt this activity to use in a range of subject areas or with different age groups. Your students could:

✓ Act out some scenes from the market in a drama session.
✓ Design and create signs to show what the different stalls sell.
✓ Use your market for a role play based in different parts of the world, selling the appropriate foods or goods.
✓ Learn and use specific words or phrases in a target language, related to buying and selling.
✓ Use this as a numeracy or maths activity, looking at buying and selling, using money, calculating profit.
✓ Set up the stalls as a small business venture with a business studies class.

Bring this activity to life by getting your students to set up some real stalls in your setting, for instance selling drinks at break times.

Using resources

Resources bring the learning to life: students love them, especially anything that's out of the ordinary. When you bring in an inspirational resource this can impact on behaviour, because it engages your students and hopefully encourages them to focus on the activity. In the Foundation Stage, the practitioner facilitates learning through the way that she resources the space – the children can only access what is made available to them. But resources are important for students of every age. Even adults love to handle something while they learn. As well as choosing the right resources, to get the right results you need to think about using them in an imaginative way.

Resources come in all different shapes and sizes:

- Natural or 'found' objects
- Man-made objects, such as toys
- Equipment – rulers, blocks, balance beams
- Paper, cardboard, collage materials
- Paints, pens, other mark-making equipment
- Props, and other 'dramatic' items
- Costumes, wigs, hats, make-up
- People – support staff, visitors, experts, other students
- Displays
- Sound and lighting – soundtracks, torches
- Cameras and other ICT equipment.

Treat your resources in a creative way. A cardboard box could be:

✓ Turned into a spaceship – decorate it, play inside it, do the count-down for 'blast off!'
✓ Presented as a 'magic box' – the students must cast the right spell to open it
✓ Designed to be the box for a fantastic new cereal
✓ Taken apart to look at how it's constructed
✓ Filled up with smaller items, to do work on volume and estimating.

As well as giving resources to your students, you can also use them yourself. Dress up as a famous figure from history or as a character from a book. Use resources to inspire your students and make them forget all about misbehaving.

PART THREE

The Students and the Setting

8

The students

Dealing with different types of student

This chapter is dedicated to understanding more about the students you work with, whether they are young children, primary-aged pupils, secondary students, teenagers, young people or adult learners. You'll find out more about why they misbehave, which strategies you can use to stop this happening, and which approaches will help you deal with misbehaviour when it does occur. You'll also find lots of case studies, designed to bring each situation to life and to show you how the ideas could work in a real-life situation.

Every student you teach is an interesting and complex individual. To an extent, though, it is possible to make some general observations to help you deal with difficult behaviour. Increasingly, the policy of inclusion means that you will come across a very wide range of students in mainstream classrooms. Some will have fairly high-level behavioural problems that in the past would have been dealt with in a specialist setting. The more you understand about the different needs that your students have, the more confident you will feel about working with them in the most effective way.

Why do students misbehave?

There is a range of complex reasons why a student, or group of students, might misbehave for you. Often, it's not just one factor contributing, but several. Let's take a look at some of the possibilities:

Factors from outside the setting

- Parents had a negative experience of school themselves, and have passed on this negativity to their children.
- There is little or no support for learning in the home.
- There are bleak prospects on offer beyond education in the area.

Factors from inside the setting

- The ethos of the school or college is ill-defined – there's a sense that chaos reigns and students can do what they want.
- The senior management team is ineffective.
- The behaviour policy is not working effectively.
- Sheer weight of numbers of difficult students, or of those with serious behaviour issues.

Factors relating to the teacher

- He regularly 'winds up' the students and gets them over-excited.
- He is vague and uncertain about the behaviour he wants to see.
- He is rude to the students, seeing them as less deserving of respect than the teacher.
- He overreacts to minor issues, turning them into confrontations.
- He is bad-tempered or moody.
- The lessons are dull, uninspired and boring.
- The activities are at the wrong level, so students can't access them.

Factors related to the student

- He has learning difficulties, and finds it hard to access the work.
- He has behaviour-related special educational needs (SEN), and finds it difficult to behave appropriately.

- He lacks motivation to learn, or has never learnt the skills of self-discipline and focus.
- He has been taught that learning is boring or meaningless.
- Negative peer pressure has a powerful influence within the group.
- There is low self-esteem, either for individuals or in the group.
- They want to wind you up – and they know that they can!

Student case studies

To help you deal more effectively with your individual students, I'm going to offer you a range of case studies. (I've alternated the gender so that they cover a balance of male and female students.) In each case study:

- I give an example of a particular 'type' of behaviour.
- I explore some of the reasons this misbehaviour might occur, including the SEN which the behaviour could flag up for you.
- I use a case study to show the kind of problems you might experience with this kind of student.
- I suggest strategies to try when working with the student from the case study, and generally when working with students who have this type of difficulty.
- I use examples from a variety of age groups.

Case study: the distracted student who lacks focus

The student (early years)

Jenna is a sweet child, but she finds it very hard to stay focused on an activity or task. When you sit with her she can concentrate for a little while, but as soon as you move away she gets distracted. You sometimes spot her staring out of the window, lost to the world. Jenna finds it particularly hard to sit still for carpet/circle time. Unless an adult sits with her, she often just wanders away. She doesn't speak very much and her language skills seem quite delayed.

What causes distraction/lack of focus?

- Never being shown at home how to focus on one single activity for an extended period
- Too many toys in the home, or too few
- Not much experience of playing together with others (carers, friends)
- Physical factors – tiredness, not eating enough, or eating the wrong things
- Too much screen time – lots of TV or computer games
- Behavioural special educational needs.

Specific strategies for helping Jenna

✓ Encourage Jenna to develop her focus. When you speak to her, hold eye contact and use plenty of tone to engage her.
✓ Pay her individual attention, greeting her by name when she arrives at your setting. Have a task and target for arrival time. For instance, her parents or carers could help her self-register, and praise her when she achieves this.
✓ At carpet time, get a member of staff to sit with her to help her focus. Alternatively, give her a little 'task' to do, such as setting out the cups for drinks.
✓ Work out where Jenna's strengths and interests lie, and set up some activities around these areas to appeal to her and boost her motivation.
✓ Do some short 'focus' activities with the group, for instance playing statues or practising physical skills such as balancing.
✓ Incorporate visual methods into the approaches you use with Jenna – pictures to show your setting routine, toy boxes labelled with photos.
✓ Speak to Jenna's parents or carers to explain how they can support Jenna at home.
✓ Get your special educational needs co-ordinator (SENCO) to observe Jenna's behaviour to see whether she has a particular learning or behavioural difficulty.

General techniques for helping distracted students

✓ Examine your lesson planning to make sure the class doesn't have to listen or focus on one task for an overly long time.
✓ Give the student something to fiddle with (a pipe cleaner, some plasticine) when you do have to talk to the whole class.
✓ Offer volunteer tasks that keep the student active and involved.
✓ Use plenty of kinaesthetic and hands-on approaches in lessons.
✓ Divide the work up into short activities. Set time limits for each one, with rewards for completion of each task.
✓ Ensure that the student understands the task – make time for a short one-to-one so she's sure of what to do.
✓ Find a responsible partner or friend with whom the student works well, and ask the helper to help her stay on task.
✓ Use an egg timer to give the student a visual aid when doing a task. Ask her to raise a hand once the sand has run through, so you know to go and check on her.
✓ Build up the length of time of tasks, as she gradually develops her focus.
✓ Use visual indicators to help the student understand the passing of time. For instance, an individual timetable with coloured symbols, stuck to the student's desk.
✓ Speak to SEN staff and get their advice. Could the inability to focus be a symptom of an unidentified special educational need?

Remember, if the student starts to misbehave because she is easily distracted, this is the ideal strategy to use. Divert her by offering an exciting alternative.

If your student has been identified as having Attention Deficit Disorder (ADD) or Attention Deficit Hyperactivity Disorder (ADHD), take the time to do some research. Some students with ADHD will be taking medication, usually a stimulant such as Ritalin, to help control the symptoms. If the symptoms are severe, the student might have a statement of special educational needs.

Many of the strategies in this book will automatically be

beneficial for students with a deficit disorder. Techniques such as using clear routines, applying boundaries consistently and setting well-structured tasks are all part of helping your student cope with her condition.

Remember: students with ADHD will not always have had their condition recognized. Sometimes, they are labelled as 'difficult' and 'disruptive' when actually these misbehaviours are happening as a result of the student's special needs.

Case study: the student who doesn't understand

The student (*lower primary*)

When Sam arrived at school he spoke very little to staff or other children. He has just moved into your Year 2 class. He is speaking a bit now, but his writing is very poor and he can only just write his name. His reading is also weak and he gets very frustrated when he can't work out what a word says. He disrupts whole-class carpet time by annoying the child sitting next to him on the carpet, or getting up and wandering around the room. When asked a question by the teacher, Sam looks blank and refuses to answer.

What causes lack of understanding?

- Various special educational needs can lead to a lack of understanding, particularly those needs that are related to communication, language and literacy.
- It could be that a young student does not understand your vocabulary; perhaps an older student cannot read what you write on the board.
- Maybe the student just hasn't had the stimulation he needs at home – if no one talks to him or reads with him, the school is going to have to put a lot of time into developing his language skills.
- Students with English as an additional language (EAL) might speak little and find it hard to understand the teacher.
- It could be that the student has a physical disability which has not been diagnosed – he can't see the board or he finds it hard to hear what you're saying.

Some students are adept at covering up difficulties with literacy. They misbehave to avoid having to show their lack of understanding and become known as being 'difficult'. This becomes a vicious cycle. The student misbehaves because he doesn't understand; because he's misbehaving, he doesn't access the learning. The longer this goes on, the more entrenched the situation becomes.

Try the following strategies with Sam:

✓ Speak as a matter of urgency to your SENCO and Sam's previous class teacher. Find out exactly what his learning needs are.
✓ Read his individual education plan (if he has one). If he doesn't, flag up your concerns with your SENCO.
✓ Create differentiated tasks, and suitable activities, so that the learning is at a level Sam can access.
✓ Where possible, give Sam one-to-one support to help him access the learning.
✓ Ignore low-level attention-seeking misbehaviour from Sam. Ask yourself, 'is this immediately interfering with my ability to teach the class?'
✓ Use clear, simple language with Sam and speak slowly. Back up what you say with hand signals.
✓ Set straightforward targets for Sam, and create an individualized reward system for him. Reward every step to boost his confidence.
✓ Consider using a scheme such as 'Reading Recovery' to bring Sam's reading up to speed.
✓ Use plenty of discussion activities: the more Sam's speaking develops, the more confident he will be about his writing.

General techniques for helping students who don't understand

✓ Use differentiated activities to give every student a chance to succeed in your lessons.
✓ Use ICT to help students – if a student finds handwriting or spelling very challenging, writing on a laptop can be helpful.
✓ Flag up concerns as soon as you have them. Don't hold back on doing this – many students go through school with an

unidentified difficulty. Once it's identified, they can get the help they need.

✓ Be conscious of the student's emotions: never embarrass him or draw attention to a particular weakness in front of the class.

✓ Make allowances, but don't excuse all misbehaviour as being caused by lack of understanding. You won't do your students any favours if you don't set them clear targets and boundaries.

✓ With adult learners, be aware that they might have a very negative experience of education, particularly if they struggled at school and didn't get the help they needed.

✓ Find a chance for your student to shine – everyone is good at *something*. Find out what that something is and let your student express his talents.

✓ Keep yourself up to date with best practice by going on training courses whenever you can.

Case study: the student who lacks motivation and interest

The student (*upper primary*)

Cassie just can't seem to be bothered. She rarely completes any work, despite being sanctioned. If she does finish something, it is scrappy and of poor quality. She regularly 'forgets' to bring her kit for PE. When questioned as to why she hasn't completed a task, Cassie will say, 'I couldn't be bothered, Miss' or 'It was boring'.

You've tried using rewards to encourage Cassie, but she doesn't respond to the usual rewards which work with other students in the class. The only time you've ever seen Cassie really enthusiastic was when a nature group visited school with some exotic insects. Her picture of the praying mantis won a prize in an art competition.

What causes lack of motivation and interest?

– Some students just aren't that interested in school, probably as a result of the parents or carers not seeing any value in education.

– As they approach secondary-school age, some students move into the hormonal roller coaster of puberty, and this has an effect on their energy and motivation levels.

- If a student isn't eating or sleeping properly, this can cause an apathetic approach.
- Some students will disguise their lack of understanding by saying that they 'can't be bothered', when what they really mean is they 'can't do it'.
- If the teacher lacks energy, is cynical or has got into bad habits, this can mean that individual students or a whole class become switched off in the lessons.
- Sometimes school is actually just a bit boring!

Try the following strategies with Cassie:

- ✓ Check with your SENCO to find out whether Cassie has any learning needs: perhaps she is covering up a difficulty.
- ✓ Make sure it's not something simple – have a chat with Cassie and her parents about whether she is eating and sleeping properly.
- ✓ Set Cassie short, achievable targets during lessons. Draw a line on the page and ask her to write down to it.
- ✓ Give her an instant reward, such as verbal praise or a sticker, every time she meets a target.
- ✓ Talk to Cassie about which rewards would actually motivate her – adapt the school system to suit her needs.
- ✓ Try to give Cassie some one-to-one support. Talk her through exactly what she needs to do and reinforce how well she is doing.
- ✓ If appropriate, sit Cassie with a well-motivated partner or friend who can help and encourage her.
- ✓ Find out what really interests Cassie and incorporate some of this into your lesson planning.
- ✓ Find something where Cassie can gain a feeling of success. Ask her what she enjoyed about the insect visit and think about how you could replicate this.
- ✓ Art seems to be an interest for her – capitalize on this to motivate her, for instance by asking her to help you create a display.
- ✓ Let Cassie use a laptop to write on for some activities. Try this as a motivator for completing a specific amount of written work.

General techniques for helping students who lack motivation

- ✓ Make the learning the driver to get your students motivated.
- ✓ Use creative, imaginative and inspirational approaches.
- ✓ Maintain a relentlessly positive approach yourself, modelling the kind of ambition and high standards you want your students to achieve.
- ✓ Put as much energy and enthusiasm as possible into the way that you deal with the class.
- ✓ If it's a whole class that seems unmotivated, it is hard to stay positive. But it's far better than the alternative: giving up and letting negativity win.
- ✓ Think about the pace of your lessons. Move quickly into the session, using your voice and body to suggest energy and forward motion.
- ✓ Every time you organize an activity, be really clear about the target for how much work should be done, and how long the students have to complete it.
- ✓ Choose short time limits and targets over longer ones, to inject a feeling of pace.
- ✓ Think about the overall look of your room – a bright and fresh space can help push us into having more get-up-and-go.
- ✓ If your overall setting is dull, drab or dilapidated, make your own teaching space an oasis of colour and delight.
- ✓ Do something original and daring and completely new with the class. Think laterally and come up with something really out of the ordinary, to show your students that education is worth it.

Case study: the aggressive and confrontational student

The student (lower secondary)
Les is a real problem around school. Other teachers frequently refer to his aggressive and antisocial behaviour in their classes. He is a large, powerfully built boy, and you often feel physically threatened by him. At the slightest provocation, Les starts to shout and cause problems. He acts very negatively towards the other members of the class, and they are becoming scared of him.

You've been warned not to contact the home because his parents also have a reputation for aggression.

Les rarely does any work in your lessons, but when you try to sanction him he reacts in a hostile manner. You've tried giving him rewards, with some success, but Les very quickly drops back into a confrontational manner.

What causes aggression and confrontation?

- Most students who are aggressive or confrontational have learnt this behaviour from their upbringing.
- If the adults in their lives always model aggressive behaviour and reactions, the child picks this up and copies it.
- Some students let off steam in school or college, because they would be too afraid to do this in the home. The teacher becomes a safety valve for them.
- Some students find it hard to manage their anger, and have never learnt strategies for self-calming.
- Other students have poor impulse control, and a tendency to respond in an emotional way.

Try the following strategies with Les:

- ✓ Check whether Les has been assessed as having special educational needs. Find out from SEN staff what sets him off.
- ✓ Arrange some anger management classes for Les. Let managers know that a number of staff feel threatened by his behaviour.
- ✓ Talk to Les (or the whole class) about different ways to manage anger and emotional reactions. Simple things like counting to ten or breathing deeply are a great help.
- ✓ Don't confront Les: it's not worth the risk to your own safety.
- ✓ Try to remain calm and use low-key approaches. Ignore minor misbehaviour as appropriate.
- ✓ Create a 'get-out' option for Les: if he feels he is going to blow, arrange for him to go and sit with a senior member of staff.
- ✓ Perhaps staff react to Les's size and physical presence and expect him to cause trouble. Avoid focusing on Les and the problems he creates for you.

✓ Document all incidents involving Les, especially if he threatens or uses aggressive or violent behaviour. Pass on copies of this information to managers and special needs staff.

✓ If you feel things are getting out of hand, and you are in danger of being assaulted, discuss this with a senior manager or union representative.

General techniques for helping aggressive/confrontational students

✓ Offer a calm, consistent and positive role model from which the student can learn.

✓ Greet the student by name at the start of lessons; mention your positive expectations of what he will achieve.

✓ Be as consistent as is possible about your expectations, but apply flexibility when it proves absolutely necessary. Don't put yourself in danger.

✓ Avoid shouting – this exacerbates confrontational behaviour.

✓ Catch the student behaving well and praise him for it. Don't wait for a negative incident to focus on him.

✓ Set achievable targets for work or behaviour and reward the student for completion of each one.

✓ Consider seating arrangements – it might be best to seat this student as close to your desk as possible.

✓ With a particularly aggressive individual, have a back-up plan whereby you remove yourself and others from danger.

In recent years, the government has clarified the law surrounding the use of reasonable force by teachers and staff working in schools. Read up on this information. Put yourself in a position where you know what you can and cannot do. Then, when a student says to you, 'you can't touch me!' you'll be able to explain exactly why his behaviour means that, in the law, you can.

Visit the government website for your local area to find advice and documents you need to read. Particularly helpful is any guidance on the use of force to control or restrain pupils.

Case study: the student with social issues

The student (upper secondary)

Sally is a strange student, newly arrived at the school. You see her wandering around the school alone at break- and lunchtimes – she doesn't seem to fit into her peer group at all. Her uniform is tatty and dirty, and you've heard students teasing her about needing to use deodorant.

Although Sally's individual work in your lessons is of a good quality, she finds it hard to work in a group. None of the other students really want to work with her, and a few of them have approached you to request that you stop putting her in their group.

When you talk to Sally individually, she finds it hard to make eye contact, and she mumbles her answers so that you can hardly hear her. Sally is not doing anything 'wrong' as such, and her behaviour is worrying rather than disruptive. Her strange behaviour is starting to have an impact on the atmosphere in the class.

What causes social issues?

- Some students find it hard to socialize and get on with their peers. Often, this will be because they have not had the experience of doing this in early childhood.
- Some special educational needs, such as being on the autistic spectrum, can cause difficulties with learning social skills and understanding social situations.
- Social issues might also be related to neglect and child protection concerns.
- At times of transition, students have to fit into new social groupings, and this can lead to peer-group issues.
- In some schools, there is a culture of negativity towards students who work hard and behave well. This can mean that some students don't fit in.
- Bullying can also be a factor in these circumstances.

Try the following strategies with Sally:

- ✓ From the evidence in the case study, it sounds as though Sally might be experiencing neglect. Speak to the school's child protection officer to flag up this possibility.
- ✓ For a while, hold back a bit from activities that require group work. Aim to get Sally settled into the class as a priority.
- ✓ Try to find out whether there is any bullying going on here. Follow the school's procedures for identifying and dealing with bullying.
- ✓ Where you do use group work, have a culture whereby you insist that everyone works with everyone, despite any personal preferences. Don't give in to those students who are complaining.
- ✓ Make it clear generally that you are not willing to put up with any bullying, and that everyone in the class must be given equal respect.
- ✓ Build up Sally's confidence, praising her by using written comments when she does a good piece of work. Try not to let other students witness the praise: they may see this as further reason to isolate her.
- ✓ Spend time talking to Sally individually during lessons, gradually winning her trust and getting her to learn how to make eye contact. Coax her gently as she is clearly fragile.
- ✓ See if you can identify one or two kinder members of the class who might be able to befriend Sally and work with her in a small group.

General techniques for helping students with social issues

- ✓ If the situation warrants it, talk to the class generally about how important it is to accept and respect anybody and everybody. Don't mention any individuals by name, just talk about how horrible it must feel to be left out of a group because nobody likes you.
- ✓ Do whole-class personal, social and health education (PSHE) activities around bullying and friendship issues. Make it completely clear that you will not accept any incidents of bullying in your class. Talk about suitable sanctions for those who do bully.

✓ If you have a group of students who don't fit into their peer group, they might appreciate it if you offer a volunteer task which allows them to stay in at break. This could be tidying a cupboard or organizing some displays. For students who are ostracized from the main bulk of the peer group, break times can be lonely and frightening.

✓ Look for ways to boost the confidence of students with social issues or low self-esteem. Encourage them to get involved in extra-curricular activities, finding something that they enjoy. This could be a debating society, a poetry club, a school or college show, The Duke of Edinburgh's Award, helping run a club for younger students, and so on.

Case study: the student who is deliberately disruptive

The student (*further education*)

Paul is a nightmare to teach! When he does turn up (always late) he immediately disrupts your lesson. He winds up the other students or gets them to join in with him in messing around. He acts aggressively towards the quieter members of the class. He rarely does any work, and when he does complete a task you often find it contains rude, personal comments about you.

When you try to sanction Paul, he responds negatively, swearing at you and insulting you. You've been in several arguments with him, and he always wants the final say. He's already told you that he's only in college for the maintenance money. You're reaching breaking point, and feeling like you want to call in sick on days when Paul is in your lesson.

What causes deliberately disruptive behaviour?

- Often, a number of factors come together to create disruptive behaviour, particularly where it is deliberate.
- Typically, the student has not done well early on in school (perhaps there are underlying learning needs which have not been identified or dealt with properly).
- It's likely that the student comes from a home background where boundaries are inconsistent or non-existent.

135

- As he progresses through school, failing and getting in trouble, it's understandable that the student feels he is a 'marked man'.
- He learns to live up to his reputation and gets some measure of satisfaction from winding up the teacher.
- He values his status within the peer group, and again gets satisfaction from being able to control or even turn the group against the teacher.
- Sometimes the teacher feels and perceives the misbehaviour as deliberate, when actually it is part of a larger SEN issue.

Try the following strategies with Paul:

✓ Document everything – write an account of the day, time, what Paul said and did. Photocopy what you've written and send copies to all the relevant people. Include the student support team, your line manager, your faculty manager, and so on.
✓ Check with college SEN staff to see whether there is something specific about Paul's background or learning needs that you should know.
✓ Follow your college disciplinary procedures to the letter, even if that means that Paul will get removed from your lessons. Don't feel guilty about this: some students (especially at this age) are beyond helping. Why should you have to put up with this rude and insulting behaviour?
✓ Ask other staff about suggestions for dealing with Paul. Find out what, if anything, is currently being done to help him change his behaviour.
✓ The rest of the class are probably fed up with Paul as well. Before he arrives, talk to the rest of your students about what they could do to help him improve. Suggest that they ignore his poor behaviour and focus on their own learning instead.
✓ Catch Paul being good (if it ever happens). Public praise might be useful here, especially if he responds well to peer-group approval.
✓ Don't get into arguments with Paul. Be the one to walk away, rather than trying to reason with someone who won't listen.
✓ Don't hesitate to bring in a senior member of staff to help you

deal with the situation if necessary. If it comes to the stage where you feel personally threatened, call for help immediately.

General techniques for helping deliberately disruptive students

✓ Accept that there are some students who make it their job to wind up the teacher and disrupt lessons. Feel pity for them, but don't waste your energy getting angry with them. You can't change the world for every single student.
✓ Follow your school or college procedures to the letter, staying calm and rational throughout (there's no *point* in allowing yourself to get wound up).
✓ Blame the policy, not the student – keep it depersonalized.
✓ Focus on what you are there for – to teach.
✓ Contact parents or carers if they are likely to be supportive. But be careful – often the student's behaviour is a result of his upbringing and contacting the home could make things worse.
✓ Don't take this type of behaviour personally, or allow it to make you become defensive. Typically it is not personal, but a reaction against an education system that the student feels has failed him.
✓ Do what you can to help, but don't let this student drain all your energy. Focus on the good, hard-working, positive students instead.

Students and special educational needs staff

These days there are many special needs staff working within the education system, all of whom should be happy to help you deal with the needs of your students. Depending on the size and type of your organization, you may have:

− A special educational needs co-ordinator (SENCO)
− Special needs assistants
− Support staff
− Educational welfare officers
− Student support officers.

Your setting will also be working in conjunction with many other agencies and professionals, including:

- Educational psychologists
- Speech therapists
- Social workers
- Child protection professionals.

Get to know these people: ask for help or for more detailed information on individual students. Sometimes confidentiality means they can't be too specific, but they can certainly give you general advice on what works best. Let other professionals know when the advice they gave you worked well for you.

As a teacher/practitioner, you are vital because you work day to day with the students. It is your role to flag up any students whose needs have not yet been identified. Students can develop behavioural difficulties at any time in their education: keep a constant eye out for any students who are experiencing problems.

Some teachers have a member of the SEN staff working in the classroom. Certainly many primary teachers now have at least a part-time teaching assistant to support them. If this is the case for you:

✓ Plan ahead to make the best use of support-staff time.
✓ Share your lesson plans in advance.
✓ Ask for help in adapting activities to suit individuals with particular needs.
✓ Ask how support staff want to work – perhaps withdrawing a few students from the class, working with groups, or with specific individuals.

Students and transitions

There are various transition points for students during their education. For instance, they might move:

- From home to a preschool or nursery

- From nursery or preschool to primary school
- From the Foundation Stage to the more formal Key Stage 1
- From infant to middle or junior school
- From primary to secondary school
- From secondary school to sixth form or college.

Around each of these points, students can experience issues with behaviour, whether it's to do with handling the change, or with moving from one situation to another, very different, one. Their learning can also suffer, either standing still or even dropping back. At transition points, students have to:

- Find their way around a new place
- Get to know new people (both staff and other students)
- Get to know the layout of the buildings
- Understand how this new setting runs
- Learn systems and routines.

This lack of knowledge about school systems means that they are more malleable, and can be moulded to your way of thinking, behaving and working. By the time they reach the last year of any setting, however, students are at the top of the heap. Their increased status means that they often begin to test the boundaries. Visit the companion website for more thoughts on how students behave at different points during their education.

9

The teaching space

The environment and behaviour

Think for a moment about how the space you live in affects the way you feel. If your home is busy, cramped and noisy, you get stressed more easily. People get under each other's feet and feelings run high. If you live in a cluttered, untidy and dirty environment, you can feel depressed and mentally overcrowded as well. If, on the other hand, you live in an open, spacious, light and airy space, with a wonderful view, this inevitably puts you in a positive, relaxed and happy mood.

From the moment they first arrive at your room, your students will be making conscious and subconscious judgements about what to expect from you, simply by what they first see of you and your space. You want to create the feeling of a calm, positive, ordered environment, where the teacher is in control. While there is much about our teaching spaces that we cannot change, there are many ways we can improve how our rooms look and consequently the behaviour of our students within them.

The way your students behave is affected by:

- The way your teaching environment appears
- The way you set out and structure the space
- How the 'stuff' within the space is organized
- How you move around the space.

See also Chapter 4 – 'The effective teacher' – for lots on how you can use your space to manage behaviour. In this chapter I look mainly at ways in which the physical environment of the classroom can be used and improved to have a positive impact on behaviour. As well as helping you handle student behaviour, your classroom should also help you stay calm, happy and relaxed.

Please note: I use the term 'space' in this chapter to describe the whole range of different teaching spaces – from classrooms to halls, drama studios to gymnasiums, lecture theatres to labs.

Improving the environment

Your students should perceive your room as a safe, calm place where learning can and will take place. If they do, they will be more likely to focus on learning and less likely to misbehave. If you teach in the early years or the primary sector, this is the place where your children will spend the majority of each session or day. Similarly, if you teach older students, this is the place where you will spend a lot of your time. Each class that visits you there should find you in control of a wonderful 'haven of learning'.

Some settings are modern, well-designed, open, airy spaces, full of light and well maintained. Others are dingy, old fashioned and run down. Whatever your teaching space is like, you owe it to yourself and your students to improve the environment as much as you can.

To get the best behaviour, work to make your space:

✓ Welcoming
✓ Tidy and uncluttered
✓ Well organized
✓ Well resourced
✓ Clearly defined
✓ Comfortable and safe
✓ Fun, colourful, engaging, multi-sensory
✓ Personal to you.

Let's look at each of those points in turn.

✓ **Welcoming**: first impressions count. Make a good visual impression using signs and displays. 'Welcome' your students and their parents in different community languages. If you have your own room, put a sign on the door with your name, class and subject as appropriate. View your room through the eyes of someone completely new – what would they notice first? What would they say was untidy or unwelcoming or missing?

✓ **Tidy and uncluttered**: a tidy environment helps you have a tidy teaching style. You (and your students) can find what you need easily, and this leads to a feeling of calm, control and relaxation. A tidy, uncluttered space gives your students the perception of order and structure, which in turn helps you build routines.

✓ **Well organized**: in an early years or primary space, set up 'stations' for different areas, putting resources in clearly labelled drawers so they are easy for students to access. Include pictures as well as words on your labels. At secondary, have a specific place to store textbooks and exercise books. Train your students to begin the session by retrieving their learning materials.

✓ **Well resourced**: keep your resources really tidy too – set aside time to sort through them regularly. In the early years, where there are plenty of toys and other resources to find space for, aim for quality rather than quantity, wood not plastic. Open-ended resources, which allow for creative thinking and many uses, are always preferable to ones with only one purpose.

✓ **Clearly defined**: clarify the different areas in your room. In an early years or primary setting, activities from different subjects can happen in different parts of the space (mark-making, art, role play, etc.). Create a clear divide between these different spaces, 'zoning' the area to help you control the children, particularly if they are at work on a number of subjects at one time. The divide could be created by using:
  - different colours
  - different types of floor covering
  - screens or a barrier
  - signs and displays
  - tables and resources.

✓ **Comfortable and safe**: look at your furniture and consider how comfy your students are when they're learning. Where possible, ask that the setting invests in good-quality seats, cushions, carpets. If you work with young children or very challenging students, ensure your environment is completely safe. Have clear rules about bags and other equipment at the start of lessons. Make sure it's safe for you as well. Ensure that effective risk assessments are in place, and speak to the named health and safety representative if you have any concerns.

✓ **Fun, colourful, engaging, multi-sensory**: think imaginatively to achieve this. Music, lights, sound, costumes, plants, displays: experiment and see what happens! Consider whether all your students' senses are stimulated when they are in your sessions, and if they're not, do something about it.

✓ **Personal to you**: bring some personal touches into the room – a favourite plant or photo, an important memento. Give your students a little insight in you the person, as well as you the teacher.

Some thoughts on displays

When I go into schools and colleges to deliver training, it always amazes me how I can get an instant 'feel' for the place, simply through what is on the walls. Displays can send a subtle but definite message that the staff and students really care about the setting. Equally, they can send a very clear message that no one here can be bothered.

No matter how poor the general condition of your classroom, you can always cheer it up with displays. In fact, displays are a good way of covering up dirty walls or peeling paint. I saw a marvellous display recently, where the teacher had got her students to paint a dramatic war poetry display directly onto the class wall (check with your managers first, though!). Used properly, displays are also great for developing your students' learning, or for rewarding hard work. The best displays have some of the following qualities:

Interesting
Brightly coloured, three-dimensional

Creative in their use of space
Stuck on windows, pegged on a 'washing line' across the ceiling

Interactive
Questions to answer, Post-it notes to add, lift-up flaps, textures

A work in progress
The 'working wall', where the students add to it as they learn
Related to the learning that's currently happening

Tidy and well cared for
Demonstrate respect by replacing pins or Blu-Tack and repairing rips

Changed regularly
Not wallpaper!

Learn to delegate the task of preparing displays: not just to a teaching assistant if you have one, but also the students. They'll be better motivated to take care of displays if you involve them in their creation.

The layout of the space

Room layout has a strong effect on students' behaviour and learning, and on their perceptions of what will happen inside the space. Depending on your age range and the subject(s) you teach, you might have to decide how to set out desks and chairs, or stools and lab benches, or perhaps a whole range of furniture and equipment in the Foundation Stage or primary classroom. You can, of course, change the layout of the space for different types of activity, getting the students to help you move furniture about.

Here are some thoughts about how students perceive different layouts, and their potential impact on learning and behaviour. In these examples I've assumed a teacher working in a classroom with desks and chairs.

The desks in rows

Advantages

- ✓ Perceived as 'traditional' by both teachers and students
- ✓ Can be a 'safe option' if you're having trouble controlling behaviour
- ✓ It is relatively easy to spot chatter or low-level misbehaviour
- ✓ The students can all see the board
- ✓ Resources, books, etc. can be passed along the rows
- ✓ This layout also makes it easier to draw up a seating plan.

Disadvantages

- ✗ Perceived as 'traditional' by both teachers and students
- ✗ It is difficult to do group work with the desks set out this way
- ✗ There is a tendency for the teacher to ignore students at the ends of each row, because they are out of the line of sight
- ✗ This set-up favours the 'chalk-and-talk' method of teaching, with teacher-led lessons
- ✗ When moving around the class, the teacher can only work with one pair of students at a time.

The desks in groups

Advantages

- ✓ Encourages a 'modern' teaching style
- ✓ Exploration and group work can happen more easily
- ✓ The activities are likely to be more student based/student led
- ✓ The teacher can talk to a whole group at a time
- ✓ It is likely that she will move more freely around the room during the lesson.

Disadvantages

✗ It can be harder to control behaviour
✗ If the teacher can't see all the faces, the students can get away with chatting and plotting misbehaviour more easily
✗ It can be harder for the students to see the board
✗ The students may view the teacher as less traditional/strict
✗ This perception could also lead to behaviour problems.

A useful alternative to the two layouts described above, is to put your desks in a U shape. This layout maximizes the advantages of both rows and desks – you can see all the faces, but equally there is still that element of control.

Some thoughts on different spaces

Teachers work in a vast array of different spaces, depending on the age range they teach and the subjects in which they specialize. Each of these spaces has its own natural advantages and disadvantages when it comes to managing behaviour.
Make sure that you:

✓ Are aware of the positive and negative aspects of your space
✓ Consider how to maximize your control over behaviour within the space
✓ Take steps to exploit the advantages of your space or spaces
✓ Equally, look for ways to minimize any difficulties you might encounter.

Below you'll find a description of different types of teaching spaces, thoughts on their advantages and disadvantages in relation to behaviour, and some top tips on utilizing each space to its best potential.

The classroom
With its fairly fixed arrangement of seating and desks, the classroom is the classic teaching space that we all know from our own school days.

Upsides:

- ✓ The desks/chairs give a sense of control and order.
- ✓ The students are sat in one place (in theory!) so are easier to manage.
- ✓ There is less opportunity for physical disruptions from students.
- ✓ The teacher can usually see all the faces when she's addressing the class.

Downsides:

- ✗ The students may feel physically restricted, and look for alternative outlets for their energy, particularly if they are restless or lack self-discipline.
- ✗ Some students may rock back on chairs or throw things across the room to a friend.
- ✗ Students who find it difficult to sit still might get up and wander around the room.
- ✗ If the room is small it can feel cramped with desks/chairs.

Top tips for managing behaviour in this space:

- ✓ Make it a priority to keep students in their seats.
- ✓ Have 'stay seated at all times' as a key rule.
- ✓ Train your students to raise their hands and wait if they need help.
- ✓ If a student does need to get up, insist she asks permission.
- ✓ Talk about *how* you want your students to sit – teach good 'sitting behaviour'.
- ✓ When addressing the class, ensure all faces are turned to you, with students attentive and ready to listen.
- ✓ For restless individuals, use 'staying in your seat' as a target, with rewards for achieving this.
- ✓ Offer outlets for those with lots of physical energy: both something to 'fidget with' and an active teaching style.
- ✓ Consider incorporating a 'movement' time during sessions.

✓ Don't be afraid to move desks and chairs around to adapt the layout.

The Foundation Stage space

This might be a unit, a purpose-built nursery or a community hall. It's typically an open space, with zoned spaces for different areas of learning. There are lots of resources and toys. The children will probably have direct access to an outdoor space.

Upsides:

✓ Because there are less desks and chairs, early years spaces often feel 'open' and spacious.
✓ The children can work at different levels, sometimes on a carpet, sometimes at a desk, sometimes standing up.
✓ The children can move quite freely around the space, accessing resources as they wish.
✓ Practitioners will often create a bright, colourful space for their children, with lots of lovely displays.
✓ If there's purpose-built accommodation/furniture, storage and organization within the space is made simpler.

Downsides:

✗ Because the space is more open than a classroom, there is the danger that children will run around the space.
✗ The practitioner needs to carefully consider all the potential risks to the children within the space.
✗ With child-initiated learning, the practitioner needs to keep a full overview of the space at all times, so she knows what all the children are doing at any time.
✗ Because there are lots of resources on offer, there's a danger that these will get 'trashed' by more challenging students.

Top tips for managing behaviour in this space:

- ✓ Use furniture and equipment to define the space and control behaviour. For instance you could add a table and chairs in an area where the children tend to run.
- ✓ Ensure there aren't any 'hidden' places where you might lose sight of the children.
- ✓ Keep a count of the overall number of children within the setting, and do regular headcounts.
- ✓ Have a very clear policy about where staff are positioned, particularly if you are free-flowing between inside and outside.
- ✓ Take good care of resources, and insist that the children are involved in tidying and sorting them.

The science lab

This space has fixed benches, high stools and a fixed teacher's desk at the front. There are cupboards for storing materials/equipment.

Upsides:

- ✓ A lab can be a fun, exciting place for students to learn. The learning is often hands-on and practical.
- ✓ There's interesting equipment to work with, and fascinating experiments to try.
- ✓ At secondary level, a science teacher often has the services of a departmental technician, to help set up equipment.
- ✓ With fixed benches, students can't create disruption by moving furniture around.
- ✓ With students facing the front, it's easier for the teacher to teach any practicals.

Downsides:

- ✗ It's harder to do group work in a lab with fixed furniture.
- ✗ There are lots of potential dangers here, particularly if the students are not well behaved.
- ✗ With gas taps, Bunsen burners, etc. there are lots of opportunities

for the students to mess around. Any misbehaviour could be potentially very dangerous indeed.

Top tips for managing behaviour in this space:

✓ Try not to shy away from practical work if you teach in a lab. This is the type of learning that students really enjoy.
✓ Teach your students through experience how to conduct experiments in a safe and sensible way.
✓ Be willing to suffer a few stressful practical lessons before they are properly trained in using the equipment.
✓ At the same time, don't put them in danger. If they refuse to behave, then remove the privilege of a practical.
✓ Make sure your class is facing the front, looking at you, and concentrating fully, before you address them.
✓ Talk through safety rules fully, and refer back to them regularly.
✓ Use 'being allowed to do practicals' as a reward for good behaviour and full attention.
✓ Keep temptation away from students as far as you can.
✓ Make it clear right from the start that you will not stand for students messing around with gas taps and Bunsen burners.

'Open' spaces
Your 'open' space might be a drama studio, a gym, a hall; it could have equipment or a raised stage area. Some newer schools and colleges have been designed specifically so that these open areas can be created.

Upsides:

✓ This is a wonderful, spacious environment for learning.
✓ Your students have a greater degree of freedom to move around.
✓ They are less likely to feel restricted or restless.
✓ Lessons in open spaces are often those that students enjoy (generally the less academic areas of the curriculum).
✓ Typically, there's less focus on writing and books, and more on physical expression.

Downsides:

✗ The sight of a big, open space may offer your students an over-whelming temptation to run around.
✗ It can be difficult to pull the class back together into one part of the space.
✗ There may be high levels of noise during the lesson, making it difficult for the teacher to regain the students' attention.
✗ If the teacher wants to do written work, it can be hard to access chairs, desks and materials.
✗ Students may resent being asked to write in practical subjects, because they don't see them as involving this kind of work.

Top tips for managing behaviour in this space:

✓ From the first time you meet your students in an open space, make it clear that the learning will be fun and exciting.
✓ Set very clear expectations of behaviour and self-discipline.
✓ If appropriate, line the class up before they enter the space.
✓ Have a 'gathering position', such as a circle, for whole-class teaching and taking the register.
✓ Use the sanction of not doing a practical lesson as a way of controlling the class.
✓ Use clipboards to do written work, book the group into an empty classroom, or do written tasks for homework.
✓ Agree a 'silence command' for when you need the whole class to pay attention. Get students to practise responding to this quickly.

The outdoors

Your outdoor space might be a tarmac playground, a grassy field, a garden or nature area. You could have access to fixed equipment, such as climbing frames, outside, or areas for different sports. Some lucky settings even have a farm area!

Upsides:

✓ There's a wonderful sense of freedom, openness and light.

✓ It's great to breathe in the fresh air.
✓ The students are 'freed up' from the confines of the typical indoor learning space.
✓ You can explore the natural environment, and make fascinating discoveries.
✓ You can make more mess without worrying – young children particularly love getting wet and muddy!

Downsides:

✘ The weather might not be great, and learning could be less than comfortable.
✘ If it is wet or cold, your students will probably complain.
✘ If you have to teach outside, you might not be too happy when it's inclement weather.
✘ Similar issues apply to those within an open space indoors – the students can see the freedom as a chance to let off steam and mess around.
✘ In an open space, it's harder to project your voice so that students can hear.

Top tips for managing behaviour in this space

✓ If you are normally based in a classroom, move your students outside to re-energize and inspire them.
✓ *Before you head outside*, make it very clear what the rules are, and what will happen if the students do not follow them.
✓ Agree a 'silence command', so that you can get your students' attention when you need to, without having to shout.
✓ If the students do mess around, or behave in a dangerous way, be clear that you will take them back inside immediately.
✓ With younger students, keep a constant check on numbers. Do a headcount before you go outside, and do it again when you go back in.

The teacher within the space

The way that you use your teaching space can help you achieve control of behaviour. Remember: your students look at the way you set up the room, and move around within it, to help them make decisions about how they will behave. Use different techniques according to the age of your students, finding ways to:

✓ Mark it as your territory
✓ Make them feel welcome
✓ Show that you're in charge now
✓ Show that positive, interesting things will happen here.

To mark the space as your territory:

✓ Meet your students outside the space – greeting them on your terms not on theirs.
✓ Create a physical barrier between the class and the room, by positioning yourself in front of the door.
✓ Ensure appropriate behaviour before you allow them into the room, making your expectations clear.

To make them feel welcome:

✓ As you allow the students in, greet them in a positive manner.
✓ Use first names as soon as you get to know them.

To show that you're in charge now:

✓ If another teacher was here previously, give clear visual indicators that it is now yours: striking displays, a change in layout.
✓ Don't get stuck at the front: move around the space in a dynamic way. Visit all the students in the course of the lesson.
✓ Occasionally change the layout of the room – an element of surprise keeps a class on its toes.

To show that positive, interesting things will happen here:

- ✓ Sometimes, use the space in an unusual way. Sit on your desk or stand at the back of the room to read a piece of text.
- ✓ Use vertical space as well as horizontal – up and down as well as side to side. Crouch beside students to chat, sit them on the floor for a story, or stand on a desk to declaim a poem.

Dealing with problem spaces

Teachers sometimes have to deal with a 'problem space' – one that is so difficult to work in that it affects the behaviour of their students. You might teach in an old, rundown school where the paint is peeling off the classroom walls. You could have to cope with a gym that is split into two for PE lessons, with only a flimsy partition to separate you from the other class. Your room might have a huge bank of windows on one wall, making it freezing cold over the winter and boiling hot in the summer months.

My first-ever secondary classroom was the classic 'problem space'. The room was tiny, and I had some large classes who would fill the space to bursting point. There were doors at either end of the classroom, and because the room linked two areas of the school together, it was seen as a useful corridor. The room was so long and narrow that some of the students had difficulty seeing the board. There was no room for movement once the classroom was full. The room would become progressively hotter as lessons wore on, particularly on summer afternoons when the sun shone straight into the room through windows without any blinds.

Unfortunately, it is a sad fact that you may be 'stuck' with a problem space, for a whole year or even longer. Use the following advice to help you minimize the issues you face.

In a noisy space

- ✓ Find ways to reduce the overall noise level of your lessons.
- ✓ Keep your teaching voice low and controlled, encouraging your students to stay quiet to hear you.

✓ Use a silence signal to get whole-class attention, but choose one that involves minimal noise, such as raising a hand.

✓ Encourage students to manage their own noise levels, for instance having a 'noise monitor' or creating a 'noise-o-meter'.

✓ Divide your lessons into 'noisy' and 'quiet' times. Follow periods of noisy group work with time for quiet reflection.

✓ Have 'time-outs' from noise: periods when the class must work in complete silence for 5 minutes or so.

In a very hot or cold space

✓ Check that the space meets the legal minimum temperature for the work place.

✓ In a very hot space, insist that your managers supply you with fans and other ways to cool it down.

✓ Don't suffer in silence – get the health and safety or union representative involved.

✓ If sunlight is an issue, ask that blinds be fitted.

✓ Be aware of how heat can affect your temperature, and the motivation levels of your students.

✓ Dress appropriately for the temperature, and encourage students to do the same, even if that means bending the rules on uniform.

In a very cramped space

✓ Consider the overall layout and experiment with alternatives.

✓ Do this particularly at the start of the year, before your students arrive.

✓ A paper plan can help you to explore the options without having to move all the furniture.

✓ Experiment with putting your desks in groups rather than rows: this generally takes up less space.

✓ Consider whether turning the entire layout to face another way would improve things.

✓ Ask for shelves to be put up on the walls, so you can store stuff without adding to the issues with space.

✓ Find ways to take your students out of the space to work on a regular basis, for instance to the playground, hall, library or an ICT room.

10

The setting or school

The setting and behaviour

There are many reasons why students misbehave – often completely unrelated to your skill as a teacher. Schools, colleges and other educational settings are a very particular kind of environment: one that can either encourage good behaviour or lead students to see poor behaviour as acceptable. If you work in a setting with a strong, positive ethos, this will contribute to the good behaviour you get in your classroom. If you work in a setting where behaviour is a problem, you might blame yourself when external factors are at least partly to blame.

Develop an awareness of all the factors governing your students' behaviour, as listed below, so that you're less likely to get stressed and defensive when they do mess around. Take steps to minimize any negative effects and try to be a part of changing the situation at your setting for the better. Let's look at how the buildings, the ethos and the management might influence behaviour within your setting as a whole.

The influence of the buildings
As we saw in the last chapter, our surroundings have a strong impact on the way we feel and behave. In schools and other settings, this can turn into a vicious cycle:

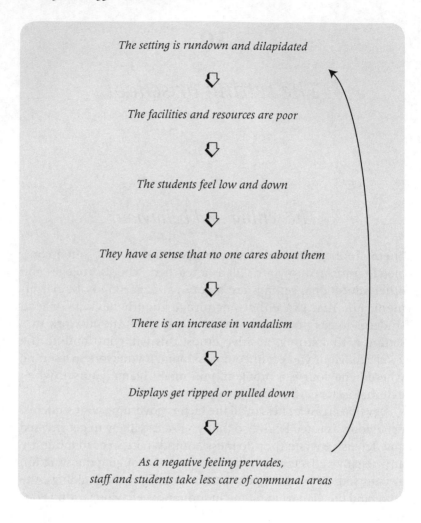

The setting is rundown and dilapidated

⬇

The facilities and resources are poor

⬇

The students feel low and down

⬇

They have a sense that no one cares about them

⬇

There is an increase in vandalism

⬇

Displays get ripped or pulled down

⬇

As a negative feeling pervades,
staff and students take less care of communal areas

If you find yourself in this situation:

✓ Make your classroom a sanctuary for your students – with plants, music, lovely scents.
✓ Put up colourful displays, so that as soon as they walk in, they are pulled into a positive frame of mind.
✓ Refuse to give up – if someone rips a display, stick it back together and put it back up again.

✓ Organize a group of volunteers to brighten up one area of the school or setting.
✓ Create a new garden or nature area outside, to show what can be done with a little effort.
✓ Don't let the overall negative atmosphere pull you into negativity. Be the shining light, leading the way with your positive aura!

The influence of the ethos

The overall 'ethos' of your setting will have a strong impact on behaviour in your classroom. It's a tricky concept to define, because it's as much about the 'feel' of the place as anything else. It basically refers to the prevailing culture, the way that the students perceive the place where they are educated.

With a positive ethos:

✓ The students behave well, in lessons and around the school.
✓ There is a culture of hard work and self-discipline.
✓ Working hard is viewed as a positive, not a negative, thing.
✓ When new students arrive, they pick up on this culture.
✓ There are lots of good role models – staff and students.
✓ The well-behaved, hard-working students outweigh the difficult.
✓ Staff have the time and energy to support individuals.
✓ Students and staff feel happy and positive about being there.
✓ Staff stay in post longer, which in turn leads to better continuity.

With a negative ethos:

✗ A culture of poor discipline prevails.
✗ Negative attitudes to learning win out over more positive ones.
✗ The 'sheer weight of numbers' makes it hard for staff to control behaviour.
✗ There is a lack of positive role models to lead change.
✗ When new students arrive, they quickly pick up on the chaotic approach.

✗ Teachers feel negative about their work and are likely not to stay in post very long.

✗ This in turn leads to students feeling that the teachers 'don't care' and consequently playing up for new staff.

Unfortunately, once the ethos of a school becomes negative, it can take years of work to put things right. As an individual there are some steps you can take to help change the ethos of your school or setting. Turn your teaching space into a place where the negative ethos cannot penetrate, and in turn you will contribute in a small but crucial way to the slow process of change.

If lack of continuity of staff is a big problem at your school, you can make a big difference simply by staying in the post for a time. This is tough in a school with a negative ethos: it will be a daily struggle against negative attitudes and the stress caused by difficult behaviour. You have to make a decision for yourself, about whether you are willing to push on through to 'make a difference' or not. Don't feel guilty if you can't, but if you are willing, remember that your choice will make a big difference for your students.

The influence of the management

The way that a school or setting is led or run has a significant impact on the behaviour you experience in your lessons. The ideal is for staff and students to see:

✓ A strong leadership team, who work closely together
✓ A keen focus on supporting and developing staff
✓ A sense that staff are highly valued
✓ Backup and support for your work in the classroom
✓ A commitment to follow through on behaviour
✓ A consistent approach to the application of sanctions
✓ A case of 'what we say, goes'
✓ A level playing field for all – not one rule for teachers and another for senior staff
✓ Managers who are highly visible around the buildings.

Unfortunately, for the average teacher, there's not much to be done when the managers are ineffective. Essentially, most teachers choose to either:

- Put up with them, and have a good moan in the staffroom when they're not there.
- Become a 'thorn in the side', making a fuss about what isn't working and generally irritating them.
- Leave a school or setting, because the management is so weak.
- Go for promotion, on the basis of 'if you can't beat 'em, join 'em'.

Effective behaviour policies

An effective and well-thought-out behaviour policy is an invaluable aid in helping you control behaviour in your classroom. Different settings have different and specific behavioural problems, depending on the age and type of students. To really work, the policy must be linked to the particular situation you face. A good policy will offer you:

- Lots of motivational rewards
- A number of potential sanction levels to work with
- An 'ultimate sanction' for crisis situations
- A system of backup beyond the classroom
- Effective methods of support for students with SEN
- A way of 'keeping tabs' on the overall behaviour of an individual (particularly within a secondary school or college, where he might be in lessons with a variety of different members of staff).

To be really effective, your policy should:

- ✓ Be created in conjunction with those staff working *in the classroom*, and include the views of non-teaching staff as well.
- ✓ Give a feeling of ownership to those people who must use it, rather than being written by someone else and then handed over.

163

✓ Undergo a continuous process of review and change, reflecting the fact that the population of the setting changes over time, and therefore so must a policy.

✓ Be consistently applied, so that students know what to expect if they misbehave *whoever the member of staff they misbehave for.*

✓ Have clear rules, clear sanctions, and an emphasis on the positive.

✓ Be realistic in what it asks you to achieve. Consistency often falls down when managers are over-ambitious in what they ask staff to achieve. For every rule, managers should consider *why you want your staff to impose this and whether it is worth the effort involved in terms of learning.* If insisting on ties is going to create conflict for staff, why not have a uniform without a tie?

✓ Involve the students too. So often, policies seem to be written without thinking about the students who are going to be asked to follow them. You might involve your students in deciding how the policy should work, perhaps by using school council representatives to put forward student views.

It is also useful if students (and their parents or carers) are asked to physically 'sign up to' the policy of the setting. Most settings will now send a home/school or home/setting contract to parents, to be signed and returned. This needs to be more than a paper exercise to really be effective. A great idea I've seen for this is where the teacher has a behaviour contract that all his students sign, and this is displayed on the classroom wall.

Below is a description of a typical whole-school behaviour policy, to show you how and why it might be effective. If you feel that your school behaviour policy is not working particularly well, you might like to suggest including some of the following ideas to help improve it. You will usually have the opportunity to do this through the meetings structure in your school.

The 'rules'

You might have two sets of rules to work with – a set within your behaviour policy, and a second set for your individual classroom. The first set outlines general behaviours expected around the school, the second is that list of expectations that you share with your students in the first lesson. The rules in your policy might refer to:

- How students should work
- What behaviour is expected in the classroom
- What behaviour is expected around the buildings
- How staff and students should behave towards each other
- How the environment and the equipment should be treated.

Of course, the way that rules are phrased varies widely according to the age of the students.

Put a laminated set of rules on your wall to refer to as you reward or sanction your students. A good set of rules will:

✓ Be short, clear and simply worded
✓ Be phrased in a positive ('do this') rather than a negative ('don't do this') way
✓ Give a sense of teamwork – 'we' rather than 'you'
✓ Make the teacher's life easier, so he can get on with teaching
✓ Not be petty or unrealistic to achieve.

Sanctions

Within the policy, there should be a system of sanctions which build up gradually. This might mean:

- A verbal warning
- A written warning
- A short punishment
- A longer or more serious punishment
- A referral.

With a gradual build-up of sanctions, the teacher can maintain control and avoid confrontation. There should be chances for the student to decide to cooperate, but the sanctions should not take too long to apply. It's important that these graduated levels are used consistently across the setting, or students get mixed messages. Those staff who do apply the policy consistently should not be seen as overly strict or unfair.

The 'ultimate' sanction

Most schools now have an 'ultimate' sanction, whereby a situation that has gone out of control can be retrieved, usually by removing the student from the classroom. It could be that a student is becoming physically violent, or simply that the teacher cannot continue teaching if the student remains in the room.

In these instances there would normally be a senior teacher available to come and remove the student. The class teacher typically sends for help by using a 'red card' or a special slip. This is taken by a reliable student to the office or reception, to summon a senior teacher. Unfortunately, it can be the case that teachers send for help and no one turns up, thus undermining the teacher and the power of the sanction.

The ultimate sanction offers a 'fallback' position for when behaviour becomes completely unacceptable or even dangerous to the teacher and other students. It should not be used as a way of repeatedly removing tricky students from the classroom. For it to be effective, the teacher must not feel worried about using it and what people might say. Equally, though, it must only be used when it is really necessary.

Behaviour units or pupil referral units

Some schools (mainly secondary) now provide a specialist unit on-site where students with repeated or severe behavioural problems can be taught. Referrals can be part of a system of sanctions; for instance, when a student reaches a certain point in the disciplinary policy, this could result in time spent in the behaviour unit.

These units are (or should be) staffed by teachers experienced in dealing with behavioural issues. The unit should have a high teacher to student ratio, so that individual attention is given to each student's needs. The eventual aim of time spent in a referral unit is to reintegrate the student back into the classroom, rather than to keep them tucked away in what used to be termed a 'sin bin'.

Effective support systems

When you have difficulties in controlling behaviour, what you most need are good support systems: someone you trust enough to share your worries with, or someone who can give you specialist advice on an issue. By its very nature, teaching is usually a fairly solitary occupation: working in your classroom you have little idea about what is going on elsewhere in the school. It is easy for the imagination to run riot, and to start thinking that all the other staff have perfect behaviour in their classrooms, to imagine that it is only you who 'can't get the buggers to behave'. Poor behaviour can make you feel depressed and alone; with an effective support system in place, you always have someone to turn to if in need.

Other teachers/staff

Because the job is so physically and emotionally taxing, teachers often develop strong bonds with their colleagues. The tougher the school or setting, often the stronger the bonds between staff. Find time to go to the staffroom during your day. Other teachers can support you by:

- Being there for you to 'let off steam' and have a moan
- Giving you tips, advice and strategies
- Helping you maintain a sense of perspective
- Understanding what you're going through
- Suggesting something that works with a particular individual.

Support staff

Increasingly, there are members of staff other than the teacher within the classroom. Although their key role is to support learning, inevitably, as part of this, they can help you manage behaviour as well. Perhaps the best use of support staff's time is in helping those students whose learning needs lead to issues with behaviour. If a student messes around when he struggles to understand an activity, get your teaching assistant to help him access the learning.

Special educational needs staff

The special educational needs staff within your setting should be an invaluable resource for you when dealing with difficult behaviour. They have specialist knowledge about the problems you are experiencing, and will also be aware of some of the background factors that cause the behaviour you face. Get to know these members of staff, and approach them for information and advice.

Managers

Some managers are a helpful source of comfort and even inspiration. As with any staff in a school, though, the truth is that some managers are effective and others less so. Staff in a management position will have at least a few years' experience. If you are relatively inexperienced, they can advise you because they've probably already encountered many of same problems when they were in the classroom full-time. Staff in management positions have a certain level of authority with students, by virtue of their position in the hierarchy. Hopefully they can use this authority to help you manage behaviour, for instance by saying (in front of a class) that you can refer any particularly troublesome students to them.

Parents and carers

Many parents and carers are genuinely keen and willing to support the work that teachers do with their children. Often, though, they have little idea of how to actually go about doing this. If an individual is causing you problems, talk to his parents or carers about what's going on. Sometimes, parents are unaware of exactly what their children are doing at school. (After all, how many students are going to confess their misbehaviour when they arrive home?) This is especially so at secondary and college levels, where there is relatively little contact between the setting and the home.

Of course, sometimes the parents or carers of your most difficult students are part of the problem, rather than part of the solution. In these instances, check with senior staff before getting in touch with the home, as this could raise child protection issues.

To get your parents working with you and supporting the work you do with your students:

✓ Give them information about what goes on in your classroom.
✓ Invite them in to see what your students have achieved.
✓ Let them know how they can support learning at home.
✓ Explain the kind of volunteer tasks they can do to assist you.

The teaching unions

Your union representative can be an excellent source of support, particularly if you are facing severe issues with behaviour. There may be health and safety concerns involved. There might also be accusations flying around from disgruntled students, when you challenge their difficult behaviour. If a student does make a complaint, get advice from your union representative about your legal position and your rights.

11

Managing behaviour: early years and primary (3–11)

Young children's behaviour

Although the vast majority of the advice I give in this book applies to students of all ages, there are strategies which are best suited to handling the behaviour of students at specific stages in their school life. In this chapter you'll find tips and techniques for those of you who are working in the early years or primary sector (3–11 years). You'll also find some examples of scenarios involving different types of problem behaviour common at this age, so that you can learn more about what to do, and what not to do.

Please note: in this chapter, because I'm dealing only with the youngest, I use the term children rather than students. I don't, however, refer to very young children or babies.

Some key principles apply when working with young children:

– Remember that an early years setting or primary school may feel like a confusing and even frightening place for them.
– Very young children are still closely attached to their parents or carers; learning to be confident and independent is key at this stage.
– Young children are very much at the beginning in learning personal, social and emotional skills, such as empathy and managing

their anger. For the early years practitioner, developing these skills is just as important as other aspects of learning.

- At this stage, the pattern for the rest of the child's educational career is being set.
- This is the chance to set good habits, patterns and routines, rather than negative ones.
- The ideal is to model good behaviour, give clear boundaries and use plenty of rewards.
- We should avoid scaring young children into behaving well, and rather aim to encourage them by using positive approaches.
- Any interventions made now will have a much greater impact than those used later on.
- Because the practitioner or teacher spends much more time with the individual children, she can have much more of an impact than with older students.
- For children from a background of poor parenting skills, the early years or primary teacher may be the first adult to model 'good' behaviour.
- A child who has never been taught about boundaries may take time to settle into the routines of the setting.

Starting out: early years settings

Children often arrive at early years settings in dribs and drabs, rather than in one whole 'year group' (this may be different for you if you teach a nursery class in a school setting). Your first few days and weeks are as much about getting to know individuals, as about getting to know the whole group. Remember:

- ✓ The children will be nervous and unsure – it will take them a while to build up their confidence. For many, this will be their first encounter with the world of education: work very hard to make it a positive one for them.
- ✓ Your role here is as much about helping the children settle in, and dealing with the emotional aspects of behaviour, as it is about dealing with any misbehaviour.
- ✓ Clear structures and routines will really help your children

settle quickly. The children need to know what happens at what point in the session, and where things are.

✓ If possible, it works really well to have a dedicated member of staff to deal with new starters. She can show the parents and their children around when they first arrive.

✓ Don't make assumptions about special educational needs at this stage – the children will probably be quiet, as they get to know the setting. Be on the look out for anything that is clearly worrying or obvious, but take your time to get to know the child first.

✓ Those children with speech or communication difficulties will find it hard to take in what is going on, and to communicate what they are feeling and thinking to you. Keep a special eye out for any children who have delayed speech.

✓ Don't assume that the children will understand everything you say to them the first time you say it.

✓ Make lots and lots of use of tone – you really cannot overdo it with this age group.

✓ Start to get to know each child's parents and carers – at this age, close contact with parents is key to helping the child learn and develop.

✓ Learn to ignore attention-seeking behaviour. A lot of the misbehaviour you see with young children is designed to get your attention. Train yourself to give attention to positive behaviours, and to ignore low-level minor misbehaviour.

Starting out: primary school

The first few days and weeks with a primary class are crucial in setting the pattern for the entire year. This applies just as much to organizing good behaviour patterns as it does to encouraging proper learning habits. For the primary school teacher, who works with this one class for the whole year, it is vital to create and develop good relationships with each child right from the start. It's also vital to begin building that sense of the class as a team, working together to achieve their best.

It's tempting to spend lots of time before the school year starts doing detailed planning. This is especially so if you are new to the job. You want to get ahead of yourself and get really well organized. But you've got to meet and get to know your children before you can plan effectively for them. Get a feel for the individuals, and for the group as a whole, before you dive into long-term planning.

When you start out with your new primary class, make it a priority to gather knowledge and information about the children.

- ✓ **Talk to colleagues**: in a reception class, get in touch with nursery or preschool practitioners to talk about the children's individual needs. With classes higher up the school, talk to other members of staff who have taught these children. Get some general input, but don't make judgements based only on the impressions of others.
- ✓ **Consider special educational needs**: talk with your SENCO and other professionals, to find out about any children who have particular learning, behavioural or physical needs. Get hold of any paperwork relating to the children and read it through so you know what to expect.
- ✓ **Learn the names**: the quicker you learn your children's names, the better you can control their behaviour and allow them to learn. Use displays, discussions, name games, sticky labels, nameplates for desks, whatever you can think of. When the children are at their desks, use a seating plan to learn names.
- ✓ **Get to know them**: rather than plunging straight into the curriculum, take time to get to know your children as individuals. Create learning activities that facilitate this, such as talking about 'my favourite things' at circle time.
- ✓ **Set your standards now**: this is the time to lay out your stall. You don't need to scare them into submission, but what you absolutely must do is come across as clear, confident and sure of what you need.

Teaching learning behaviours

It's really important to remember that you're here to help the children learn, rather than to manage their behaviour (although helping them learn to manage their *own* behaviour is clearly one of your learning intentions). Get the correct behaviours in place early on, and both you and they can focus on the learning. These children are going to be in education for a long time: certain behaviours need to become ingrained, so that learning can happen more easily. The younger the children, the newer these learning behaviours might be to them. Adapt the suggestions below to the age of the children you work with. You need to help them learn:

✓ **Sitting behaviour**: when they're sitting down, be fussy about how your children sit – whether on a carpet or a chair. (At the same time, be sensible about how long you get them to sit, according to their age and the kind of setting you're working in.) Get them to sit up straight, cross their legs, fold their arms, and keep themselves to themselves. Be clear about why it's important for their safety not to tip back on chairs. If you want them to ask permission before getting up, set that expectation right now. These sound like very minor issues to worry about, but there are several very important reasons to get this particular behaviour right:
  - Proper sitting tends to lead to full attention, and consequently to more effective learning.
  - It's a safety issue – tipping back on chairs is dangerous.
  - It's a health issue as well – they're going to be sitting *an awful lot* over the next however many years in education. Get them to learn to sit with good posture, to avoid back issues later on.
  - There is less chance the children will annoy each other, and consequently less chance of those irritating complaints about 'she pushed me'.
  - You send a message about who is in charge in your classroom, or in overall control of your teaching space.
✓ **Listening behaviour**: when you have to talk to the whole group you want your children to be silent and attentive so they hear and understand what is being said. Exactly the same applies when one of the children is talking in a whole-group situation. Teach good listening behaviour right from the start, and you will do your children a huge favour. If they learn how to listen properly, they really will learn so much more effectively. Use lots of eye

contact and pauses, to check that you have their full attention.

✓ **Answering behaviour:** teach your children about what you want them to do when you ask a question. Again, this is something that is going to happen throughout their school life. The key learning behaviour you're after here is that the children learn not to call out. The exact approach you go for will depend on the kind of question you're asking, the age of the children, and also on your viewpoint about what works best for learning. You might use:

– Talk partners, where the children discuss their ideas, then you ask for a response
– Direct questioning, of named individuals, with some thinking-time first, i.e. 'Charlotte, can you answer this question . . .'
– The 'hands up to answer, everyone tries to participate' approach.

Whatever your preferred approach, get the habits in place now. Use prompts to ingrain those habits, for example asking 'Put up your hand if you can tell me . . .'.

✓ **Activity behaviours:** be clear with your children about exactly how they should approach activities for learning, whether group work, discussions, writing tasks, and so on. With older children you might put a list of these up on the wall, or in the front of exercise books, as a reminder. At Foundation Stage, your list might be:

– We share
– We take care
– We take turns
– We tidy up when we're finished.

With older children, your list for writing activities might be:

– Always put a title and date, and underline it
– Write as neatly as you can
– Take time to check your work for spelling and punctuation
– Work quietly (or in silence if you prefer)
– Put your hand up if you have a question or if you need help.

To get these learning behaviours in place, you need to repeat them over and over again with your children, until they become habits. You also need to insist on what you've asked for: just as with your expectations, you must model them consistently. Once you get these things in place, your life gets easier, and you can focus on the learning.

'Training' your children

In the film *Kindergarten Cop*, Arnold Schwarzenegger trains his class of young children as though they are at 'police academy'. This fictional example demonstrates a very important point about working with young children. Train them to behave well right from the start, *and make it seem fun to behave like this*, and they will happily follow your instructions from then onwards. This should then leave you free to deal with the minority of children who have more complex behavioural or learning needs. Effectively, this 'training' involves sharing your expectations and letting the class see them in action.

You can 'train' your children in:

✓ **The morning routine**: what happens when the children arrive in the morning – what do they do first? What happens about books, and equipment, and registering? Where are you, and what are you doing at this point? At what point do they come to the carpet or settle down to an activity? Get a clear routine in place, train your children up, and the start of your day should run smoothly.

✓ **Responding to your signals**: ideally, you want the children to respond quickly and habitually to your signals, so it's easy to gain their attention. This isn't about being a 'control freak', but about creating a safe environment, and ensuring effective learning can take place. If they respond quickly, this also means far less effort expended by you.

✓ **Dealing with equipment**: train your children to collect, use and put away equipment as you want them to do it. This saves you time and effort, but more importantly it asks that they take responsibility for their own learning. Spice this up by adding a bit of competition – 'who's got the neatest drawer?' or 'who can pick up the most blocks?'.

✓ **The end-of-day routine**: get your children trained to tidy up, to tuck in chairs, to leave the room as they found it. This helps them learn responsibility, and shows them that the space and resources are of value, and are to be treated with respect.

Behaviour management doesn't have to be a really heavy and weighty thing, where you drone on at your children about how they must do this, and mustn't do that, and on and on and on. If you keep it light and use a soft touch, you can often get them to do what you want without them realizing what you're doing. To make behaving well seem like fun, you could:

✓ **Turn tasks into a 'game'**: consider the way you present tasks and activities to your children. Use vocabulary that suggests fun and challenge rather than boredom and hard work. For instance, to get a group to lie down and be still for story time, introduce this as a game of 'sleeping lions'. The children must pretend to be lions, fast asleep and very still.
✓ **Enter the world of make-believe**: children of all ages respond to make-believe (and funnily enough, so do older students as well). They love the chance to use their imaginations: the opportunity to be someone, something or somewhere they are not. For example, to get a group to tidy up the room very quietly, tell them to pretend that there's a sleeping giant beneath the floor, and they really mustn't wake him. (Particularly effective if you've just been reading *Jack and the Beanstalk*).
✓ **Treat them as adults**: another very useful fiction is that the children are much more grown up than they really are. For instance, they could play the part of a crazy science professor while doing an experiment. Foundation Stage practitioners can have great fun with this, getting the children to be firefighters, doctors, animal-rescue workers, circus performers – the possibilities are limitless! When you get your children to take on the role of an expert like this, you can use it to encourage responsible behaviour and attitudes. Interact with the children as though they are adults, expressing surprise at any silliness: 'I can hardly believe you're doing that, Professor Smith, seeing as you're a world-famous scientist.'

Seven key strategies and techniques

In Chapter 3 you read about my ten key strategies and techniques for effective behaviour management. In this section, you'll find an additional seven approaches that are particularly useful in the early years and at primary school. The seven key strategies are:

> 1 Know how to get your children's attention
> 2 Understand how to keep your children's attention
> 3 Learn how to give clear instructions
> 4 Distraction, not reaction
> 5 Take an overview
> 6 Spread your attention around
> 7 Get creative with rewards

1. Know how to get your children's attention

With young children it's important to find effective ways to get their attention, and to get it quickly if required. The younger the children, the more easily distracted they are, and consequently the harder it can be to gain everyone's attention. In an early years setting, many of the traditional structures of a classroom do not apply (children at desks, doing activities set by the teacher). There's less sense of control, but there will still be times when you do need to pull everyone together.

Your children might be:

- Totally engrossed in an activity
- About to do something dangerous
- Getting overexcited or too loud
- Moving between activities
- In the middle of a noisy discussion task.

When you need to get your children's attention, you want to avoid shouting because it stresses your voice, and in any case is not easily heard in a noisy room. Set up a 'silence signal' with your group – a signal agreed ahead of time, that tells them 'I need silence now'.

There are lots of different techniques you can try to do this:

- ✓ **The non-verbal signal:** this is effective because it doesn't add any noise to the setting. Because the children fall silent without hearing anything, it gives a sense that the teacher is in control of the situation. Your non-verbal signal might be a 'silent seat', where you sit when you want the children to come straight to the carpet. You could raise a hand to indicate that the children should stop what they are doing, fall silent, and raise their hands too.
- ✓ **The time target:** this is a useful technique for older children, because it places the responsibility on them, rather than on you. Before they start an activity, set them a challenge: while they work they must keep an eye on the clock, and at a specified time they should fall silent in preparation for the next instruction. At the appointed time you will usually find one or two of your more observant individuals 'shushing' the rest of the class for you.
- ✓ **The visual signal:** this one's great for shorter activities. Get hold of a large egg timer, or download a stopwatch onto your interactive whiteboard. When you say 'go' the children start work; when the sand or timer runs out, they must stop.
- ✓ **The targeted command:** for this signal, you do a countdown, for instance '5, 4, 3, 2, 1, freeze!'. On 'freeze', the children must freeze as still as statues. Make it into a 'game' – get your children to respond more quickly each time you play the game.
- ✓ **The sound signal:** you play a brief burst of music, give a quick whistle, ring a bell, or any other kind of interesting sound. This indicates that it's time for the children to stop what they're doing and pay attention. Those students who stop quickest could get a reward.
- ✓ **'We all join in':** start clicking your fingers in a pattern, for instance two slow clicks followed by three fast ones. The children must join in with your pattern, copying it exactly. Because they are concentrating on copying your rhythm, you'll find the children should stop talking. You can then slow down the clicking gradually, until the children all stop at the same moment.

2. Understand how to keep your children's attention

Because young children are so easily distracted, you must work hard to keep the attention of your children once you've got it. This is particularly so when you're explaining an activity or doing a teacher-led task. The older the children, the longer the stretches they will be able to concentrate and pay attention. You'll also need to ensure that they maintain their attention on activities during the course of the lesson.

To achieve this key strategy:

✓ **Keep eye contact**: as you talk to your children, keep your eyes moving around to ensure that every child is looking right at you. If you notice someone is not, pause for a moment, without saying anything. The child will usually pick up on the fact that you have stopped speaking (this may take a while), and look at you to find you staring straight at her. Don't be afraid to pause as often as is required to ensure attention.

✓ **Repeat back to me**: when you explain an activity, it's easy for children to look as though they're listening when in fact the words are not actually registering in their brains. After you've finished your run-through of what you want the children to do, get someone to repeat this back to you. With older children, choose a child who you suspect was not really listening. Clarify any possible misunderstandings before the children begin work.

✓ **Chunk up your sessions**: break up longer lessons or sessions into smaller chunks, so that you keep your children focused, rewarding them for each activity. In the Foundation Stage, you could have whole-group times, times for free choice, times for a focused activity. When you offer breaks between activities, use this as a chance for the children to 'stretch' themselves: this could be a quick 'brain stretch' (perhaps some mental maths games) or a physical stretch (such as shaking out their bodies).

3. Learn how to give clear instructions

There will be lots of times during your day when you need to give instructions to the group or class. It could be learning-related (how to complete an activity); it could be about your routine (time to wash your hands for a snack). It is hard for young children to take in all the things that are going on around them. After all, only recently their parents or carers were their whole world. Now they are in an early years setting or school, where many different things are going on around them. It's easy for them to get sidetracked.

One of the main causes of what we call 'misbehaviour' is a child *who doesn't understand what you want her to do*. She's not intentionally being difficult, it's just that she doesn't actually understand, so she can't complete the task or activity you've set. It's surprisingly hard to give good instructions: if you're new to the profession don't worry if you're finding it hard – it's a skill that comes with lots of practice.

In fact, understanding instructions seems to be an area where even adults have a 'blind spot'. When I set up an activity at a training day, I aim to give very clear instructions about the task (and obviously I'm experienced at doing this). Even so, I joke that when I set the group off on the activity, someone in the room will say 'what were we meant to do again?'.

If the children don't understand your instructions, all sorts of disruptions can arise. You set them off on an activity, only to find that five hands immediately go up, with children saying 'I don't understand what I'm meant to do'. You then have to stop everyone and explain the task over again. Those children who are not confident enough to ask for help might mess around to cover up their lack of understanding.

Overcome these issues by giving effective instructions in the first place, using the following strategies and approaches to help you:

✓ **Be clear, simple and direct**: make your instructions as simple as possible – aim them at the weakest, most confused child in the class. Speak with a slow, well-modulated voice, emphasizing key words as you talk.
✓ **Give a visual backup**: some children find it much easier to understand what they see than what they hear. Use lots of visual methods to reinforce your instructions – hand signals, diagrams, key points written on the board, props, etc.
✓ **Give an example or a demonstration**: go through examples with

the children to reinforce what you want them to do. An example helps us take an idea from the abstract concept to the concrete activity. Ask for volunteers to help you demonstrate – this helps you encourage participation and check for understanding.

✓ **Consider your language**: as adults, we use words freely, without considering the need for understanding. For young children, with a limited vocabulary, take care to ensure that every word is easily understood. Be as specific as you can: instead of saying 'take care with your punctuation', ask your children to 'make sure you put all the full stops and commas in the right places'.

✓ **Use time indicators**: to avoid an aural jumble, make the timing of what you want very clear. To clarify order, use phrases such as 'first I want you to . . .'. Set a clear time to complete the activity you've set.

✓ **Follow the 'rule of three'**: children find it hard to retain more than about three instructions at once: this is a good guide to the maximum amount of information they can process at any one time. Where possible when giving instructions, limit yourself to three main points.

✓ **Use lots of repetition**: train yourself to repeat instructions over and over again, in a range of clear, direct ways, to ensure you have complete understanding. Ask the children to repeat back to you what you said, to check for any areas of weak comprehension.

Here's a quick example of a teacher giving good, clear instructions to a Year 3 class:

'When I say go, I want you to go straight to your desks and open your exercise books. First, write the title and date. Then complete questions one, two and three from the board. You have ten minutes. Sanjay, please could you repeat what I've just said to the class?'

When you set up an activity, get help from teaching assistants and other staff. Share information about the activities before the lesson: they can help you by explaining the activity to children who don't understand.

4. Distraction, not reaction

The younger the children you work with, the less likely it is that you will need to turn to any of the higher-level sanctions described in Chapter 6. In most instances, you should hopefully be able to use a low-level approach – non-verbal signals such as a disappointed look. With your more challenging children, you might need to use a system such as yellow and red cards, or time-outs. Of course there might be some children who are so out of control that you have no choice but to push through to the bitter end. But most of the time, your main focus will be on the clear setting of boundaries, rather than on the application of punishments.

When children misbehave, one of the very best approaches of all is to offer them a distraction. At this age, children are not making the kind of conscious decision to disrupt that you might experience in a secondary school or a college of further education. Even your most disruptive children will have got themselves into the subconscious habit of being difficult, rather than sitting down one day and thinking, 'I really must disrupt Miss Smith's lesson'. When you 'react to' problem behaviour, you draw attention to it – you're also likely to lose the flow of what you were doing. When you 'distract from' problem behaviour, you deal with it quickly, and in a low-key manner.

Here are some examples, to show you what I mean:

Three years old
Charlie is wriggling around during show and tell on the carpet.
React to: the practitioner brings attention to the problem, by saying, 'Charlie, stop wriggling around and wait your turn'.
Distract from: the practitioner signals to her colleague to take Charlie away to set out some toys for when circle time is finished.

Six years old
Angie is disrupting a whole-class carpet-time session by repeatedly digging her elbow into the person next to her.
React to: the teacher makes Angie stand up, and tells her off in front of the class.
Distract from: the teacher asks her to come to the front and

help write something up on the whiteboard.

Nine years old
T. J. is walking around the classroom and disrupting others, even though the class have been told to stay in their seats.

React to: the teacher goes up to T. J. and says, 'why on earth are you out of your seat?'.

Distract from: the teacher says to T. J., 'While you're up, hand out these sheets, but then *straight back to your seat okay*. Don't make me get my yellow cards out.'

This is not to say that you shouldn't deal with a child who repeatedly misbehaves. If the child has already been told not to do something, and persists in doing it, you will need to turn to sanctions. Use the rule of thumb from the rewards and sanctions chapter (see Chapter 6): 'once nicely, once firmly, then get on with it'. Remember, too, that you should still talk to the child about any problem behaviour. Don't let it interrupt the flow of your teaching, but do chat after the event, when the rest of the class are on task, and you have the chance to talk in private.

5. Take an overview

When you work with one group or class for all or most of the time, it is easy to get pulled into fixed patterns of behaviour with them. You know the individuals so well, that you have specific expectations about how they will behave when you ask them to do something. For instance, the moment you set a task, you home in on that 'difficult' table of children; or, you trail around after Carlie during free play, because you know she always gets herself into trouble.

As well as helping and focusing on individuals, it's also important to keep a continuous overview of the class or group as a whole. What's happening on the other side of the room, while you're doing that craft activity with Helen? What are the overall noise levels like; do you need to stop the class to pull the level of excitement down a bit? It's a tricky technique to master, because you want to sit and give individual children your attention. But eventually, with experience, you learn to develop those 'eyes in the back of your head'!

When you set the whole class off on an activity:

✓ Don't move towards any one group or child immediately.
✓ Stand still for a moment, and gain an overview of the entire group.
✓ Consider: who's settling down and focusing, who looks unsure?
✓ Give a positive – 'Green table's doing great!', rather than moving straight towards any children who are off task.

Similarly, when you're sitting with an individual or small group to support them:

✓ Keep an eye out for what's happening on the other side of the room.
✓ Use non-verbal signals as required to deal with any issues.
✓ If you do speak to the class, make sure it's to highlight someone who's working well, rather than someone who isn't.
✓ Have a constant feel for how loud overall noise levels are.
✓ Have an ongoing sense of levels of excitement or conversely lack of energy/motivation.
✓ Stop the class to pull together, or to give any reminders as and when required.

Of course this doesn't mean that you should never give your full attention to one child or one group. Don't intervene with every tiny incident – sometimes, give yourself permission to focus fully on one of your kids.

6. *Spread your attention around*

If you work with a class or group where there are lots of children with behavioural difficulties, what can happen is that those children take up the majority of your time and energy. Even though you try to focus on the positive, there are so many low-level incidents of misbehaviour that you simply cannot avoid getting sucked into dealing with them. In part, this is a result of inclusion – there are simply more children with complex needs within the modern-day classroom. Although this is not the place for a debate about the merits of inclusion, what it does mean is that teachers are facing more incidents of misbehaviour, often behaviour that is challenging and hard to handle.

If this is the case for you, it can start to feel like you focus only on the difficult children. You might feel as though you are giving out loads of rewards to the poorly behaved children, and none to those who always sit quietly and get on with their learning. When you're managing behaviour, it's really important to remember:

> *Although you should support and help the minority of children who have behavioural needs, you should never do so at the expense of the majority who want to learn.*

In the day-to-day reality of the classroom, this means that you must not feel guilty about focusing on the 'good' kids. If you are using up all your energy and time dealing with one really challenging child, then insist that the school does something about giving you additional support. Be willing to ignore low-level misbehaviour, in order to focus in on helping that group who never seem to get your attention. Alternatively, push through with the behaviour policy, and if that means sending a child to a more senior member of staff because she is constantly attacking others, then that is what you must do. Aim to spread yourself around as equally and as fairly as you can, so that all the children get the benefit of time spent with you.

7. Get creative with rewards

In early years and primary settings, you can have great fun getting creative with rewards. Show your children that *behaving well is fun* and that *learning is fun too*! Perhaps the very best reward of all is a lesson or activity that is enjoyable and engrossing, and where the children really feel that they've learnt something. There's little to beat the sense of achievement of working hard and seeing a creditable end result.

When I meet early years and primary teachers, I'm always amazed at how inventive they are with rewards, particularly when creating whole-class reward systems. The point with rewards is, you don't have to be consistent like you do with sanctions. You can create your own unique and imaginative approaches, ones that you know your class will respond to. Here are a few suggestions, nicked from some of the early years and primary staff I've met over the last few years:

✓ **Deputy Diners**: the children earn the right to be a 'deputy diner' – each teacher nominates a child for this privilege. At lunch time, the 'deputy diners' sit and have their lunch with the deputy. The table is set with proper linen, a vase with real flowers, proper napkins, china plates, shiny silver cutlery. They are served at their table by a 'waiter' (the headteacher if you want to have fun!)

✓ **All the colours of the rainbow**: the teacher creates a huge 'weather' display on her wall. There are various Velcro pictures that can be attached to the display, depending on how well the children are working and behaving. The weather might be rainy, to show that she's not happy, or the sun could come out, when the class is working well. If things are going brilliantly, there is the ultimate accolade of a rainbow.

✓ **Sad/Happy Book**: this is a lovely, simple idea to show children that they have two choices around their behaviour. The child is given a book, one side with a happy face on the cover, the other side with a sad one. Happy comments go in on one side; turn over the book and sad comments go in the other.

✓ **Treasure Box**: I really liked this idea and I now use it when I'm working with teachers. You get hold of a box, something attractive, one with a key if possible. Fill the box with all different kinds of 'treasures'. My box has packs of pencils, little notebooks, packets of seeds, pots of glitter, sweets. When a child does something really brilliant, they get to dip in the treasure box and pick out a prize.

For a download listing loads of different, creative rewards, visit my website: www.suecowley.co.uk.

Towards the secondary school

By the time they reach the last year of the primary phase, students are preparing to make the transition from child to young adult. They are on the cusp of becoming teenagers. But they're not yet quite ready to shrug off some of the childlike feelings and emotions which may lead to immature and silly behaviour. At this stage, the children have an added sense of confidence as a result of being 'top dogs' in the school. Things change dramatically when they arrive at secondary school, where they are once again at the bottom of the pile.

At this age, children may start to push at the boundaries and test adult authority, as they take the first steps on the road to becoming a grown-up. Consequently, you need to adapt the strategies you use to suit these older children. When working with students at the top of the primary school:

✓ **Take them seriously**: at this age, children often see themselves as more grown up than they are. If you want them to behave in a mature way, take their feelings seriously. Never talk down to them. Treat them as the young adults they will soon be, and they might surprise you by living up to your expectations.

✓ **Offer a positive role model**: positive role models become particularly important at this age, as children start to understand that their parents are not the whole world. They start paying more attention to external influences, including their peer group and their teachers. You might invite a secondary school student in to offer them a positive example and to talk to them about what the move to the 'big school' entails.

✓ **Know what interests them**: at this age children start to take a keen interest in the wider world, and the cultural icons surrounding them in the media. They are starting to gain their independence, and their parents may be giving them more freedom to choose their own clothes and music, or to stay out later in the evenings. Stay up to date with trends (the latest TV show, the popular footballers) and find out what interests your class. Incorporate some of this into your teaching, or at the very least show that you have some knowledge about it.

✓ **Understand their fears and concerns**: at this age children become very sensitive to peer-group pressure. They may be fearful of being left out of the group, so could succumb to negative pressures to misbehave more easily. They may start to feel embarrassed about relationships with the opposite gender – be a bit sensitive to the kind of groups you ask them to work in.

Handling the transition

The transition to secondary school can be an extremely difficult time for students. They are full of concerns about what secondary school will be like. Moving from one teacher to many is also a huge change for them. Do what you can to minimize any negative effects of the transition on both behaviour and learning. Many schools now have a member of staff who has the responsibility for helping children make a smooth transition. To ease their path, you could:

✓ **Organize visits**: bring secondary students into your classroom, or arrange a visit so that your Year 6 children can go to their new secondary school. (Similarly, if children come into your reception class from local preschools, do a two-way visit to prepare them for primary school.)
✓ **Talk through the differences**: talk with your children about the differences between primary and secondary school. Give them advice on coping with having different teachers for different subjects, and on moving around the school rather than staying in one classroom.
✓ **Help them get organized**: talk to your children about how they might best organize themselves – they can do this over the summer before they start at secondary school. For example, ensuring that they have the right equipment, packing their bags the night before school, getting their uniform out and ready to put on in the morning.
✓ **Pen pals**: get your Year 6 students to make pen pals with some Year 7 counterparts in local schools. By exchanging letters, they can find out the 'truth' about secondary school. Hopefully

this will help dispel many of those rumours that amazingly still float around, such as having your head flushed down the toilet. Having a 'contact' at secondary school can also lessen the fear when they start at the new school. They will know at least one person when they arrive.

✓ **Mentors:** some schools now offer older mentors to pair up with primary students in their first year of secondary school. These mentors typically come from Year 9 or 10. Again, it is useful for young students to have a contact to help them settle in.

✓ **Shared topics:** some schools now link up to do a shared topic in the final term of primary, which then moves with the child into the first year at secondary. The Year 6 and Year 7 teachers work together to find a topic that will inspire their students.

12

Managing behaviour: secondary and further education (11+)

Behaviour with young people and adults

Although all the techniques described in this book will help you manage behaviour more effectively, there are certain approaches that work particularly well with older students. Often, it's a case of adapting the basic technique (for instance, 'be definite') to suit the age and type of the students you have. Those teachers working in a secondary school or further education college have to deal with students of all different ages. During the day, you might see preteens, teenagers, young adults, adult learners (sometimes within the same class). Learning to adapt your style to fit each of these age groups is an important teaching technique for you, requiring great subtlety and skill.

Working with older students is very rewarding – you get to teach your subject at a level that stretches and challenges both you and them. However, it can also be one of the most challenging teaching situations when behaviour is a problem. Some of your students might be physically larger than you: if they become confrontational, you may feel threatened and vulnerable. By this age disaffection with education can cause problems with motivation. Some learners at further education level will have had a particularly bad experience of school, and may project this onto you and your lessons.

At the top end of the age range, you'll be working with students who are adults, or who are almost grown up. They will have many adult concerns that are nothing to do with education. These concerns can really get in the way of their learning, and some will need a great deal of support from you and your setting, beyond what happens in the classroom. With this age range there's also all the pressure of taking and passing exams, and getting ready to move into the full-time work environment.

Starting out

The first few lessons with any class are vital in setting the scene for a successful year. For teachers working in secondary schools and colleges, the beginning of term means meeting and getting to know large numbers of people. Learning names is a real issue, especially for the teacher of a 'once-a-week' subject, who may be teaching hundreds of different students. Below I look at how you need to establish and communicate your style, set your key standards, and get patterns in place, during those first few weeks.

A question of style

With this age range, your personal teaching style becomes particularly important in getting good behaviour. What you have to decide (ahead of time) is what approach will work best with each of your classes. You need to take into account the kind of organization you're working within. If this is a tough, challenging place, full of disaffected students, you're going to have to take a different tack to the one you would take in an easier environment.

In a secondary school . . .

Your students are moving from class to class, and encountering lots of different kinds of teachers. They will be making decisions based on the judgements they make about the effectiveness of your style. Your reputation around the school will also impact on their views of you, and of how they should behave for you. Your style plays a critical part in creating a reputation for effectiveness.

In a college . . .

Your students are (mostly) there out of some measure of choice – most of them are no longer in the statutory part of their education. They will be seeing themselves as 'adult learners' for the first time, capable of making decisions about whether they are being taught well or not. Some younger college students choosing a vocational pathway will have done so because they didn't get on with the school environment.

What kind of style should I use?

In my opinion, what you're after is to be 'as tough as you feel you can get away with' – the 'no-nonsense' style if you like. You need to get the students to view you as:

✓ Firm
✓ Confident
✓ Here to make learning happen.

This doesn't mean that you 'shouldn't smile until Christmas', as the old adage goes. What I've found, though, is that students actually prefer, and respect, a teacher who works in this way from the start. There is no room for messing about: the learning takes absolute priority.

Being 'no-nonsense' does not mean:

✗ Being rude
✗ Being negative
✗ Reacting aggressively
✗ Getting into confrontations.

Being 'no-nonsense' does mean:

✓ Being certain and definite about your standards
✓ Being clear about how your lessons will run
✓ Staying calm no matter what the provocation
✓ Knowing when to bend rather than break.

Generally speaking, with the youngest secondary school students, you can play it strict: 'I'm the teacher and this is exactly what you will do in my lessons'. By the time you get to 15-year-olds and above, you need to temper the toughness with a bit of laid-back cool. Take into account their 'nearly adult' status, so it's more: 'don't mess with me guys, you'll regret it'. If you're working with adults, you'll need to use a workplace-type approach, where a manager might say: 'here's the line, just don't step over it'.

Let's take one example – getting your students into your room – and look at the way you could communicate a 'no-nonsense' style with different age groups:

11–13 years: you're standing in the doorway when the students arrive. You get them to line up outside the classroom, single file, facing front, in silence, before they're allowed inside. As they enter, you check for any uniform infringements. You get anyone who isn't in proper uniform to step to one side and sort it out, before being allowed in.

14–16 years: you're standing in the doorway, leaning against the jamb to suggest how relaxed you are. You let the students in as they arrive, dealing with any really obvious issues, such as trainers rather than shoes (in a school) or a student chatting on his phone (in a college).

17+ years: you're sat on your desk when the learners arrive. You welcome them in, glancing at your watch to indicate that you're ready to get started. Once about half the class is in the room, you stand up and move towards the door and poke your head out. You use a hand signal to show the rest of the learners that they need to get a move on. You begin to pull the door shut, to indicate, 'we're starting now'.

In some very challenging teaching situations, you'll need to tread carefully with a no-nonsense style. Make sure you come over as assertive rather than aggressive. Similarly, with some particularly difficult students, you're going to need to take a more laid-back, relaxed approach, coaxing them into doing what you want, rather than it being a demand. Do this where you know the only alternative would be a confrontational student: 'whatever works' is a good rule of thumb.

Don't feel bad about being the one in charge – someone has to be, and most of your students want it to be you. Because if it's not you, then it'll be one or more of them, and the worst behaved ones will tend to take over and run the place. And once that happens, those who do want to learn something can't, and that's the worst of all possible worlds.

Once you've got the students behaving and learning as you wish, you can make a gradual relaxation in your style. This provides you with a useful carrot – 'if I see you all working really sensibly, I'll let you talk quietly while you write'. Don't relax too soon or too suddenly, particularly in your first year of teaching. The first half-term is about the right length of time for you to communicate your no-nonsense style and to cement your reputation as a teacher 'not to be messed with'.

Setting the standards

Before you meet your classes, you've got to decide for yourself which expectations or standards are completely non-negotiable. Which things you are willing to 'fight to the death' for. I have certain key standards that I will *never* let drop: no matter if I'm teaching young children, teenagers or adults; no matter if the students are easy or the most difficult I've ever met. The day I let these expectations of behaviour drop, would be the day that I think very seriously about not being a teacher any more.

However, that is not to say that these things are easy to achieve, or that I always manage to get them. In some teaching situations they will be nigh on impossible – they will take every ounce of your energy, and then some more. But you've got to keep your aims in mind, and strive constantly to achieve them, because otherwise you've effectively told your students (in a Catherine Tate-esque style) *'whatever'*.

Your standards need to be:

✓ Realistic and achievable; but also
✓ High enough to let learning happen.

My non-negotiables would be:

✓ We *listen properly* to each other.
✓ We *respect* each other.

✓ We *do our best* for ourselves and for each other.

Remember, the way you phrase these standards will vary according to the age of the students. Here's an example of how I might phrase my first non-negotiable for different age groups. (You may well wish to phrase yours differently – remember, whatever works!)

11–13 years: *'I expect everyone to listen in complete silence when someone is addressing the whole group. And I want to see eye contact and focused attention.'*

14–16 years: *'I really need you to listen to me, and to each other, so we can get on with learning. Does anyone have any questions about that? Because it's an absolute in my classroom.'*

17+ years: *'The most important thing for me is that we listen properly – that means you listen to each other, and when I need to talk to you, you listen to me too. And you're going to listen in silence – anyone have any thoughts about why that's important?'*

When you're setting your standards, particularly at the lower-secondary age range, it's often the small things that count. If you let your students get away with something small, this sends a signal that other things are up for negotiation. For instance, you might:

✓ Insist that written work is done in silence, so they can concentrate. Offset this with the 'generous gift' of 2-minute time-outs to talk.
✓ Adhere like glue to uniform rules, such as coats off, no trainers, blazers on, ties done up properly.
✓ Stamp down on small breaches of the rules, for instance the chewing of gum.

The older the students, the more you might decide to 'overlook' very small infringements of the rules. If a disaffected 16-year-old has his tie undone, but is working, you're not going to want to bother him. But make it clear that you're 'overlooking' this rule-breaking because he is getting on with his work.

Setting up the patterns

As well as setting your standards, at the start of the year you should also set up the pattern of how your lessons will run. These patterns are especially vital where students are being taught by a number of different teachers. They need to see a well-structured, clear and consistent pattern to your lessons, so they feel secure about how to behave for you.

You can see an example of a teacher setting up a lesson pattern in Chapter 2. When thinking about the pattern you want, consider the following questions:

- What do I want my students to do when they first arrive at my lesson?
- Where am I when they arrive at the room?
- How do they know where to sit? Is this a free choice or not?
- At what point, and how, are resources and equipment put on desks?
- What do I do about taking a register, and how do the students behave while I do that?
- How do I explain the learning that's going to take place in the lesson?
- How should the students behave while I'm explaining it?
- What kind of working atmosphere do I want?
- How do we deal with resources and equipment?
- What happens to finish off the lesson?
- How do students behave while getting ready to leave the room?
- How do I dismiss the class?

Your pattern will depend on how 'formal' you want or need your lessons to be. If you're working with the youngest students in a very traditional classroom environment, you're probably going to go for a very structured approach. If you're working with adult vocational learners in a workshop setting, you're not going to want or need such a tightly controlled style.

Seven key strategies and techniques

In Chapter 3 I looked at ten key strategies and techniques for effective behaviour management. In this section, you'll find an additional seven approaches that are particularly useful in a secondary school or in a further education setting.

The seven key strategies are:

> 1 Be inventive to get their attention
> 2 Treat them as adults
> 3 But sometimes . . . treat them as children
> 4 Blame the policy
> 5 Make the learning real
> 6 Show your human side
> 7 Be an inspiration.

1. Be inventive to get their attention

When you need to talk to the whole class, you've got to have their attention. If you don't, consider the signals you're sending: basically, you're saying you don't mind them not listening to you, that you don't believe you have enough control to get them to listen, and that what you're saying really isn't all that important.

With some (perhaps many) classes in this age range, this can be a difficult aim to achieve. I too have stood at the front of a class, waiting for their attention and feeling certain that I will never fulfil my aim. I am fully aware of how nerve-racking it feels, and how tempting it is to give in and just start talking anyway, even though some students aren't listening.

There are many different ways you can get your students to pay attention, and the best strategies are the inventive, imaginative and interesting ones. Have a look at the following ideas and see which ones might work for you, or how you might adapt them to use with your classes.

✓ **Note to class:** look sad, move to your board, and write: 'If you won't all be silent and let me get on with teaching you, then unfortunately I'm going to have to turn to sanctions, and I really don't want to have to do that.' By the time you're halfway through writing that, hopefully the class will be looking to see what you're doing.

✓ **The theatrical gesture**: try this if you have a bit of the drama queen or king in your soul. At the very least, you'll get your students' attention and raise a laugh. Pretend to bang your head on your desk and start sobbing, saying 'Why oh why won't they be silent? I just can't cope anymore. Oh what am I going to do!?'

✓ **Rubbish!**: walk over to your classroom bin, pick it up and place it in the centre of the room. Step into the bin, and wait. When the students ask what you're doing, explain that: 'You're treating me like rubbish, so I thought I'd act like it too, and stand in the bin.'

✓ **Speak my language**: ask the class for a suitable phrase and response that you could use to get their attention. The teacher who originally gave me this idea told me that her inner-city kids went for the following. Teacher: *'Oyyy!'* Students: *'You wot?'*

2. Treat them as adults

Students live up (or down) to what you expect of them. Treat them like adults and you may be surprised at the mature way in which they respond. Some will let you down, but you should never let the silly behaviour of a minority prevent you from doing something with the well-behaved majority. The older the students are, the more adult the way you can treat them.

In return for you treating them as adults, they have a responsibility to behave and work appropriately. Make it clear to your students that this is a partnership: if they don't fulfill their end of the bargain, you are entitled to withdraw any privileges you've given.

To treat them as adults, you should:

✓ Give them your trust.
✓ Give them a chance to prove themselves to you, rather than assuming the worst.
✓ Let them get hands-on with equipment and resources, even if you're not sure how they will respond.

✓ Speak to them as you would to a fellow worker, if you worked in an office.

And make sure you don't:

✗ Patronize them (temper your use of tone the older the learners)
✗ Speak down to them
✗ Suggest (by your body language, vocabulary, actions) that they are somehow 'below' you.

3. But sometimes . . . treat them as children

Paradoxically, older students also respond well to the teacher who uses childlike approaches from time to time. Education at this stage can be very serious and highly pressured; it's important to let them blow off steam on occasions. You could:

✓ Play some games with them
✓ Do a fun, light-hearted quiz
✓ Set up a really messy activity
✓ Find an excuse to do some dressing up
✓ Hand out some childlike rewards – stickers, lollies, bubbles.

And when you give them the go-ahead to act like children, it'll work even better if you join in the activity too!

4. Blame the policy

The older the students, the more they tend to 'fight back' when a teacher gives them a sanction. When this happens, it can mean that:

– The teacher and student get into an argument
– The student backs himself into a corner and gets thrown out
– The teacher avoids sanctioning because he wants to avoid confrontation.

Clearly, there will be times when it is necessary to use a sanction: what you need to do is find a way to do this without getting into confrontations. To achieve this, use the technique of 'blame the policy'. Remember that your role here is not to discipline – you are here to teach. The only reason you discipline is to allow you to *get on with the teaching*. When you blame the policy, this demonstrates to the student that the behaviour is *between him and the institution*, rather than *between you and him*.

In order to be in a position to blame the policy, you need to know what the policy is in the first place. Be 100 per cent certain: know the rule on gum, mobile phones, jewellery, coats, trainers, swearing and so on and so forth. Otherwise you'll find that, when your students challenge you about the sanction, you come across as unsure and you're tempted to back down. Have a paper copy of the school behaviour policy or the college disciplinary procedures to hand at all times.

Here's a (slightly tongue-in-cheek) example of a teacher 'blaming the policy', with a college-aged learner, to show you what I mean:

The teacher has asked Mark three times to get on with some work. He currently has his feet up on the table and is staring out of the window.

Teacher:	Mark, I notice that you have ignored my previous three requests to get on with some work.
Mark:	What you gonna do 'bout it?
Teacher:	[*whipping out his copy of the college disciplinary procedures*] Well Mark, I think you'll find [*leafs through pages*] that under Clause 3, sub-section (ii) of the disciplinary policy, it says that 'Students who repeatedly refuse to comply with a reasonable request should be asked to leave the lesson'.
Mark:	[*completely confused by this*] Huh?!?
Teacher:	Mark, you have a choice. Feet down, get on with the work. Refuse to comply, leave the lesson. Up to you.

5. Make the learning real

In Chapter 7 I looked at how you can 'teach for good behaviour'. In the secondary school and in further education, one of the key features in that aspiration is to make the learning real. This is particularly important for students who are engaged in a vocational or work-based course at college. They simply have to see the links between what they are learning, and the job that they could get once they qualify.

In the secondary school, those really disaffected teenagers who cause you so much misery, often turn into totally different people when they go on a work experience placement. They begin to see how the adult world of work is out there waiting for them, just around the corner. The reward of a salary, and the freedom that having money can bring, is a fantastic 'carrot' for students of this age. Equally, though, they have to accept that misbehaviour in the workplace has a definitive outcome – the potential to lose your job.

When you 'make the learning real', you clarify and underline this link between what happens in school or college, and what happens in the adult world beyond. To 'make it real', you could:

- ✓ **Set up workplace-style scenarios**: for instance, a 'scene' from a building site, with various hazards to identify. Get the students to work 'in character' as health and safety inspectors, to find as many hazards as they can.
- ✓ **Include plenty of resources**: make the resources you use as real, and as 'hands-on', as possible. If there's an option to go for a real or a toy version of an item, choose the real item in preference.
- ✓ **Demonstrate the importance of theory**: students in this age range love being taught technical-sounding terms – my Year 7 students have loved the idea of learning about 'pathetic fallacy' in their English classes. Show how this theory links to the reality of the subject, and make 'doing the theory' a condition for 'doing the practical bits'.
- ✓ **Get out of the classroom**: some of my very best experiences as a teacher have been outside the classroom walls. Taking a GCSE class to the theatre, or a group of young children to a farm. By taking your class into the real world, you show them that education and learning are everywhere.

6. Show your human side

When you're working with older students, the approaches you use can generally be a bit closer to the edge than those you might use with children. How far you go depends both on your personal philosophies of education, and on what your setting finds acceptable. Although you want to enforce consistent boundaries, you also need to take into account that sometimes in life we want to push at and stretch the boundaries – to rebel a little against what 'authority' says we must do.

For instance, you know that your Year 9 students would respond well to being bribed with some chocolate, but your school's healthy eating policy means you're not meant to have sweets in school. What do you do? Or, your most difficult learner only ever does any work if you 'overlook' the fact that he is wearing his headphones. Again, what's the best thing to do? (There's no right or wrong answer, you have to make the professional judgement for yourself.)

You can also show that you're human by:

✓ Laughing at yourself when you make a mistake.
✓ Sharing some of your interests with students (which football team you support, that kind of thing).
✓ Giving them, as well as yourself, the occasional relaxed lesson.
✓ Sharing a few fun anecdotes from your life outside of education.

Come across as someone who is self-deprecating, particularly with older students where you don't need to maintain your 'teacher' image quite so much.

7. Be an inspiration

When you set out to work in education, I'm sure you didn't do so because you 'just needed a job'. Being in the profession is too tough to do it just for a living wage: the vast majority of us do it because we really care about making a difference. Working with students of 11 years and above, you are (hopefully) teaching them the subject that you love. Never lose sight of how lucky you are to be working all day with that subject which inspires you. Aim to pass your inspiration and your love of the subject on to your students.

When students sense that their teacher *really cares* about his subject, they cannot help but be at least a little bit interested too. Remember, some of those students sitting in front of you will one day choose to study this subject in depth, perhaps to degree level or even beyond. If you can be at least partly responsible for that decision, what a wonderful thing to achieve!

To be an inspiration, you'll need to:

✓ Put energy and enthusiasm into your teaching.
✓ Get creative with your approaches, and take some risks.
✓ Use your face, voice and body in an imaginative way.
✓ Choose a teaching style that engages or interests.
✓ Model an attitude to learning that your students can learn from.
✓ Model the kind of behaviour your students should aspire to emulate.

The form tutor and behaviour

Those of you working as secondary teachers will often be expected to take on a pastoral role within your school. As a form tutor, you register your group and take responsibility for their overall progress and welfare. Working with a form group is a very different prospect to working with a class in a subject area. In fact, you might not be timetabled to teach any of your form-group students at all.

How you handle behaviour with your form group depends on two main factors: the expectations of the school as to how form tutors should work, and the age and type of students in the group. On the whole, you can afford to take a more relaxed approach to the role of form tutor than class teacher. Adapt the style you use as a subject teacher, and develop a different kind of relationship with these students. This more relaxed relationship is important, because your form tutees may be coming to you with personal or social concerns, and they need to feel free to talk openly. When working as a form tutor:

✓ **Match your approaches to the age group**: if you are given a class of a group in their first year at secondary school, you have a wonderful chance to 'train them up' in your ways of working. Start out with a fairly firm approach, then relax a little over time. If you're given a rowdy group in their last year of schooling, who have had four different tutors over the years, there is little point giving yourself a stressful time by trying to crack the whip too hard.

✓ **Keep a check on equipment**: with younger students, help them to organize themselves properly, and to avoid pointless sanctions for missing equipment, etc. With a group who are new to secondary, you might do an equipment check at the start of each day/week.

✓ **Keep an overview of sanctions and rewards**: most schools now use diaries, where teachers can record sanctions and rewards earned. Take an overview of how well (or badly) each student is doing by looking at their diaries. If necessary provide an early alert system for more senior staff.

✓ **Sort out the issues that waste lesson time**: act as a useful support and backup for subject teachers, by sorting out those minor issues that eat into lesson time. Ensure that your students have shoes on rather than trainers, and uniform sorted, before they head off for the day's lessons.

✓ **Consider how best to take the register**: with younger tutees, you will probably be able to insist on and get total silence to take the register. With some older classes, such an approach will only set you up for confrontations. If you are likely to have difficulty getting the class silent, ask for a volunteer to help you check who is and is not present. Mark the register yourself, though – it's a legal document and your responsibility.

✓ **Keep a teacher/tutor divide**: if you teach members of your form group, you need to make it clear that the two roles are distinct. Have a quiet word with any individuals who push at the boundaries, clarifying the different roles that you play in class and in tutor time.

13

For example . . .

The examples

If you read and follow the advice in this book, you should be in a good position to deal with most of the behaviour issues you face. That's not to say you will be able to solve all of them, but you'll know which strategies might work. And if you face a behaviour issue that seems insoluble, you'll hopefully understand that it isn't necessarily your fault if you can't solve it straight away.

In this chapter you'll find some examples of the different behaviour issues you might experience, and how you could go about handling them. In each of these examples, you'll see both a 'good' way to go about handling the situation, and also a 'bad' way. There's a commentary on each approach too, to show you why the teacher's chosen techniques do or don't work. I've illustrated a variety of techniques – ignoring, distracting, setting clear expectations, and so on. Which one you would choose to apply depends on the situation and the student.

As you read these examples, please bear in mind that they only represent *one possible way* of going about things. How you choose to handle such situations will depend on your teaching style, your children, your setting, your policies, and so on. Please also bear in mind that it is hard to capture the complexities of the average student, teacher, setting or classroom in a short playscript. I make no claims to be Shakespeare, but I do hope that these examples give you some useful ideas to get you thinking.

I've chosen a whole range of potential situations, and have set them at a variety of different age levels. As with the whole of this

book, please take from this what works for you and your students,
adapting the ideas as necessary to suit the age and subjects that you
teach. In this chapter I've once again alternated male and female
students, to give variety to the scenarios.

The tantrum

Age group: 2–4 years

Details: Ella is throwing the Lego bricks across the room. Lynne,
the early years practitioner, goes across to her and asks her to stop.
A few minutes later she notices that Ella has started throwing
bricks again.

A good example

Lynne: Ella, I told you to stop throwing the bricks. Look, we
could build a tower together, shall we see how high
we can make it?

*Ella picks up another brick, looks to check that Lynne is watching, and then
throws it hard across the room.*

Lynne: That's a shame, Ella. I'm afraid I'm going to have to
take the Lego away, someone might get hurt with you
throwing it. [*She picks up the box and puts on the lid.*]

Ella: [*flips*] GIVE ME THE LEGO BACK! I WANT THE
LEGO! THAT'S NOT FAIR!

Lynne: [*moves in close to Ella and speaks very calmly*] Ella. Ella.
I need you to calm down now.

Ella: I WANT THE LEGO! I WANT IT BACK! NOW!

Lynne: Ella, I need you to calm down and stop screaming.

Ella: IT'S NOT FAIR! I WANT THE LEGO!

Lynne, deciding that Ella is not going to calm down, stands up.

Lynne: Ella, I'll come back when you've calmed down. Now,

	what's Charlie doing over here? Oh, what a lovely drawing, Charlie, haven't you worked hard on that!
Ella:	GIVE ME THE LEGO BACK!

Lynne ignores her and moves over to the art table, keeping half an eye on her to see what happens.

Ella:	I want the Lego, I want it, I want it, I want it . . . [*she starts to run out of steam*]

Commentary on the good example

When a child of this age throws a screaming tantrum, there is little point in trying to reason with her. Here, Lynne tries to distract Ella, by getting her to build a tower. When that doesn't work, she tries a couple of times to calm Ella down, but she quickly sees that this is not going to work. She decides that she will have to take the toy away. As she does, she explains that it is Ella's behaviour that is the problem, and why (rather than focusing on Ella herself being the issue). When Ella immediately throws a tantrum, instead of responding or caving in to Ella's demands, she shows Ella that shouting is not the way to get her attention. She highlights the good behaviour of another child and leaves the situation, still keeping a close eye on Ella to ensure that she is able to calm herself down.

A bad example

Lynne:	Ella, didn't I ask you to stop throwing the bricks? Why are you throwing the bricks? Why can't you just play nicely with them?

Ella picks up another brick, looks to check that Lynne is watching, and then throws it hard across the room.

Lynne:	Ella! You're being really naughty now! Well, that's it. The Lego is gone. [*She picks up the box and puts on the lid.*]
Ella:	[*flips*] GIVE ME THE LEGO BACK! I WANT THE LEGO! THAT'S NOT FAIR!

Lynne:	[*beginning to raise her voice a bit*] Well, it's your fault I had to take it. You were the one being silly.
Ella:	I WANT THE LEGO! I WANT IT BACK! NOW!
Lynne:	Look, if you promise to play nicely, maybe I'll let you have it back.
Ella:	Give it back, now!
Lynne:	Will you play nicely with it?
Ella:	Yes. Give it back now!
Lynne:	Are you sure you're going to play nicely with it?
Ella:	Yes. Promise. Oh please can I have it back [*starting to whine*].
Lynne:	Here you go, but you'd better play nicely with it this time.

Lynne moves away. As soon as her back is turned, Ella lobs another brick across the room.

Commentary on the bad example

Notice how Lynne opens the exchange by asking a series of questions, rather than by reiterating the behaviour she actually wants. Instead of trying to involve Ella in playing, she very quickly moves to take the toy away. She blames Ella directly, rather than highlighting the behaviour as the issue. She also starts to get wound up, instead of using her verbal skills to calm the situation down. When Ella starts screaming, she panics and starts to reason with her. She very quickly gives in to Ella's demands. This is a dangerous precedent to set – she has basically just taught Ella that she can get her own way by screaming!

The dangerous object

Age group: 5–7 years

Details: Rikky has been warned on previous occasions that he must not play around with scissors. The teacher has talked with the class about why this behaviour is dangerous. However, Rikky still has a tendency to wave scissors around dangerously, and in the past he has cut the other children's hair and clothes with them.

A good example
Rikky has a pair of scissors and is threatening to cut Marilyn's hair with them. She has started crying.

Marilyn: Miss! Miss! Rikky's gonna cut my hair! Make him stop!

Rikky: I'm only playing, Miss. I'm not really gonna cut her hair.

Miss Pirot: Marilyn, could you go and help Mrs Bryan get the drinks out, ready for lunch time? That's excellent, thanks very much Marilyn. [*Marilyn goes to sort out the drinks.*] Now, Rikky. I want you to give me those scissors right this minute. Hand them over. Now. [*She holds out her hand.*]

Rikky: Oh, Miss! That's not fair. I wasn't doing nothing with them. I need them to cut my maps out.

Miss Pirot: Rikky. I want you to hand me the scissors right now. If you show me how sensible you can be, you can have them back after lunch. [*She holds out her hand.*] Thank you.

Rikky: [*starting to get aggravated*] No. I won't. I can't do my work without them.

Miss Pirot: Rikky, you have a choice. Give me the scissors *now* or you will force me to give you a yellow card.

Rikky: No, I won't give you them.

Miss Pirot: Then here's your yellow card [*she hands it to him*]. Now, don't make me change it for a red one. Give me the scissors right now, Rikky.

He hands them over grudgingly.

Commentary on the good example
The teacher intervenes early to stop a more serious situation from developing. If she had left Rikky to his own devices, he might have cut Marilyn. The teacher's first step is to remove Marilyn from

the equation by offering her an exciting alternative. This will also help distract Marilyn from being upset. Next, she insists that Rikky hand over the scissors. His response, that he needs them for his work, is true, but she points out that he can have them back (a reward for better behaviour) after lunch. She says 'thank you' to try to encourage him to hand them over. Rikky at first refuses to comply, and so the teacher gives him a level-one sanction. Once he realizes she is serious, he decides not to push things further, and hands her the scissors.

A bad example

Rikky has a pair of scissors and is threatening to cut Marilyn's hair with them. She has started crying.

Marilyn:	Miss! Miss! Rikky's gonna cut my hair! Make him stop!
Rikky:	I'm only playing, Miss. I'm not really gonna cut her hair.
Miss Pirot:	Rikky. I've asked you before and I'll ask you again. Can you please stop playing with the scissors? You know it's dangerous. Marilyn, do stop being such a baby and crying like that. He hasn't hurt you, has he?
Rikky:	Oh, Miss! That's not fair. I wasn't doing nothing with them. I need them to cut my maps out.
Miss Pirot:	Can you hand me the scissors now, Rikky?
Rikky:	[*starting to get aggravated*] No. That's not fair. I won't. I can't do my work without them.
Miss Pirot:	[*shouting*] Rikky! Give me the scissors or there's no playtime for you today!

Now, both Rikky and Marilyn are crying. The rest of the class have stopped working to watch.

Miss Pirot:	Now look what you've done, you silly children! Do shut up and get on with the work!
Rikky:	I hate you!

Miss Pirot: And I hate you, Rikky! Leave the room now and go to stand outside the head's office. [*Exasperated.*] Oh, Marilyn, do stop that awful crying!

Commentary on the bad example

This time, instead of removing Marilyn from the situation, the teacher accuses her of being silly: rather an unfair charge. When Rikky refuses to comply with her, the teacher quickly becomes annoyed and starts to shout, rather than remaining calm and dealing with the problem in a rational way. She threatens Rikky without warning that he will lose his playtime, thus exacerbating his sense of unfairness.

When the rest of the class start to watch the incident, she calls both Rikky and Marilyn 'silly' and tells them to 'shut up'. This rudeness is bound to aggravate things, and Rikky responds by telling her he 'hates her'. She reacts rudely again, and the situation is only 'resolved' by sending him to the head's office, rather an overreaction to a problem that should have been easily dealt with. She is left with a class of students who are completely distracted from their work, and one student in floods of tears.

The plasticine flicker

Age group: 8–11 years

Details: Sally is a real handful. She can be very disruptive, and if she gets bored in lessons she starts to flick plasticine at the other students. The teacher doesn't always see her doing this, but the other children keep complaining, and at the end of the day, Miss Burn's carpet is always covered in little bits of plasticine.

A good example

The class are working in small groups on a weighing activity. They are weighing different substances to see which ones are heavy and which ones are light, and to record the weights for comparison. Unfortunately, one of the things that they have to weigh is plasticine. Miss Burn is keeping a close eye on Sally's group. She notices that they are about to weigh the plasticine.

Miss Burn:	Well done, red group. You've managed to weigh all these different things so far. What did you find out about them?
Ben:	The tissue paper is really light, Miss.
Miss Burn:	That's great, Ben. What else did you find out?
Robert:	The metal block was very heavy.
Miss Burn:	Excellent, Robert. What about the plasticine? Sally, do you think that's going to be heavy or light?
Sally:	Light, Miss.
Miss Burn:	Are you sure, Sally? Shall we try it now?
Sally:	Okay. [*She weighs it.*] Oh. It's heavy, Miss.
Miss Burn:	And when something is heavy, what could happen if we throw it at someone? Ben, what do you think?
Ben:	You might hurt them, Miss?
Miss Burn:	That's right. Now, Sally. Do you think it's a good idea to throw a metal block at someone?
Sally:	Definitely not, Miss.
Miss Burn:	And plasticine?
Sally:	Well, you could just throw a little bit. Then it wouldn't hurt them.
Miss Burn:	But what if it got in their eyes?
Robert:	That would hurt loads! I got some soap in my eyes and it really hurt. Plasticine might be like that.
Miss Burn:	And what would happen if we got plasticine on the carpet?
Robert:	It could go all sticky. Look, Miss, there's some on the carpet here. Uggh!
Miss Burn:	Do you think it's ever right to throw things, Ben?
Ben:	Well . . . you can throw a ball in the playground, Miss.
Miss Burn:	But what about in the classroom? What do you think, Sally?
Sally:	No. We shouldn't throw things at all, Miss.

Commentary on the good example

In this example, the teacher comes at the problem from a lateral direction. Rather than catching Sally in the act of throwing (which would have been tricky), she decides to approach the issue by discussing it, trying to make the children understand why they shouldn't throw things. She approaches the group just as they are about to tackle the plasticine, and immediately praises them for the way they are working, setting up a positive feeling about the whole encounter.

She discusses the activity with them, making sure they all contribute, and leading up to the issue of why it might be dangerous to throw plasticine. At no point does she actually accuse Sally of throwing plasticine, but what she does do is point out the problems that might be caused if anyone happened to do this. The whole issue is completely depersonalized, and Sally will hopefully be forced to reconsider her behaviour. If she does continue to flick plasticine, the teacher can simply refer back to this discussion, making clear the reasons for stopping the behaviour.

A bad example

The class are working in small groups on an art activity. They are making plasticine models of farm animals for a project. Miss Burn is helping green group when she gets hit on the head by a plasticine pellet.

Miss Burn:	Ow! Who threw that? That really hurt me. Sally? Was it you? I've seen you throwing plasticine before.
Sally:	No, Miss. It wasn't me. It was Josh.
Josh:	No it wasn't. It was you, Sally, I saw you.
Miss Burn:	Sally. Not only do you throw plasticine at me, but you're also a liar. Why are you being so silly?
Sally:	I didn't throw it. Josh is lying.
Josh:	No I'm not. You're the liar. Liar! Liar!
Miss Burn:	Stop it! Both of you! Go and sit by my desk. If you can't behave yourselves, then no fun activities for you.

Sally and Josh go to sit by her desk. A few minutes later a fight starts between them.

Miss Burn: STOP THAT RIGHT NOW!

Commentary on the bad example

This encounter seems doomed to failure right from the start. Because the teacher has just been hit by the pellet, she is emotional about the situation, rather than approaching it in a calm and rational way. Her immediate reaction is to accuse Sally. Although she may well be correct in doing this, it does seem unfair to blame her without any proof. Sally, probably embarrassed about her behaviour, tries to lay the blame on another student. Josh understandably feels aggrieved about this. He is then sanctioned despite having done nothing wrong. The incident ends with the children being punished, but the punishment deprives them of the chance to do their work. It would be far better to sanction them in a way that does not impact on their learning, but instead makes them address their behaviour.

It is hardly surprising that a fight starts between the two children when they are sitting by Miss Burn's desk, bored, with nothing to occupy them. They are watching the others do a fun activity, and for Josh in particular this must seem very unfair – all he did was defend himself when he was falsely accused!

The talkative class

Age group: 11–12 years

Details: although this class is generally good natured and well behaved, they can be incredibly talkative. This is causing Miss Flynn problems, particularly at the start of the lesson when she wants to settle them down, take the register, and get on with the work.

A good example

The class arrive for their lesson, chatting away happily. Miss Flynn is standing at the door, blocking the entrance, arms folded, looking mean.

Miss Flynn: Right! Today we're going to line up before we come in the room. I want to see how quickly you can line up in silence. Five . . . four . . . three . . . two . . . one . . .

The class are now lined up, but the students are still chatting among themselves. Miss Flynn coughs and looks at her watch, but doesn't say anything. She waits a moment to see whether they will become silent without any intervention, but they continue talking.

Miss Flynn: [*apparently talking to herself*] Oh dear. They're not silent. And that's what I want before I let them in the room, because I need to talk to them. Oh well, it looks like they're going to be spending some of their break time with me. What a shame. And they're such a nice class, although they are just too chatty. [*She sighs and looks at her watch.*] That's 1 minute wasted, so that's 1 minute at break time.

The class realize what is going on and the more observant students 'shush' the others. There is still some low-level chatter, though.

Miss Flynn: [*looking at her watch again*] Well, some of them are listening, but that's still 2 minutes wasted. Of course, I might allow them to win the time back if they can all be silent in five . . . four . . . three . . . two . . . one . . . zero!

It works! Miss Flynn can now address the class and let them into the room.

Miss Flynn: That's excellent. Well done. Now, that is how we are going to start every lesson from this point onwards – lined up in silence, waiting outside the classroom. I've decided that you're becoming rather too talkative and I'm going to stamp it out. Right. I want you to come into the classroom quietly and sensibly. As soon as you are in your seats, I want you to get your books and pens out, and sit in silence, arms folded, so that

> I can take the register. The first person ready, sitting in silence, gets a yellow reward slip!

The class hurry inside, and by the time Miss Flynn comes in, they are all waiting in silence.

Commentary on the good example

The teacher has decided to use a fairly light approach to deal with the problem, although with a touch of strictness as necessary. This kind of style is well suited to lower-secondary students – if the teacher suddenly needs to clamp down on them, she could simply raise her voice slightly, or change her tone. When the students arrive, she is ready and waiting for them, her strategy already planned. The first thing she does is set the class a challenge, with a time limit, counting down from five to see whether this will work. It does to a certain extent, because the students are now in a straight line (useful because she can see all their faces). Unfortunately they are still chatting.

Now the teacher decides to use a rather unusual technique. She acts as though she is talking to herself, telling herself what she wants from the class, how they are failing to meet her expectations, how she does in fact really like them, and finally what the result of their continued chatter will be. By appearing to talk to herself, and thinking out loud, she depersonalizes the sanction she threatens. The students start to respond and, capitalizing on this, the teacher offers them a get-out clause of winning back the detention time. Finally, she again uses the countdown technique and this time it works.

Once the students are completely silent and attentive, the teacher can talk to them about why she wants them to line up in this way. She sets the standard for the future, so that they know what is expected of them when they come to her lesson next time. Lastly, she gives them a target to achieve, with a reward for the first to manage it (this age group generally love to compete) – to get into the room quickly and quietly and then sit in silence so that she can take the register. Notice how, throughout the encounter, the teacher remains relentlessly polite and calm.

A bad example

The class arrive for their lesson, chatting away happily. Miss Flynn is inside the classroom, doing some last-minute preparation. When she sees them starting to come in, she waves them back outside.

Miss Flynn: No, no, no! Get out! Out! I'm not letting you lot in here until you're quiet. Get back outside and wait for me.

James, a nice, quiet, well-behaved student is already sitting at his desk, getting his pencil case and books out.

Miss Flynn: James! Out I said! I can't believe it! What is wrong with you today? You're normally so nice. Pack your stuff up and get out!

James: But, Miss . . .

Miss Flynn: Don't you 'but, Miss' me, young man. Just shut up and do what I say.

More students are arriving, and Miss Flynn backs them up to the door, waving her hands at them.

Miss Flynn: Outside. Outside, I said! I want you lot lined up and silent.

The class make a vague sort of line, but there is still quite a lot of talking.

Miss Flynn: Right, shut up you lot, I want to talk to you.

James is talking to the student behind him, telling her to be quiet for Miss Flynn.

Miss Flynn: James! Didn't you hear me? I said be quiet. That's the second time you've disobeyed me today. Right. You're in detention with me after the lesson.

James: But, Miss . . . that's not fair! I was only telling . . .

Miss Flynn: Don't talk back to me. You were talking, now you're in detention. Now can you lot please shut up and let me get on with it.

By now the class are either engrossed in watching the confrontation between Miss Flynn and James, or are chatting among themselves because they are bored with waiting.

Miss Flynn: [*losing her temper*] I said be quiet! SHUT UP!

The class quietens down, although a few of the regular troublemakers are at the back, still talking.

Miss Flynn: Right, when you get inside sit down and be silent so I can take the register. Okay? Come on then, in you come.

Commentary on the bad example

Right from the start of the lesson, it is clear that Miss Flynn is not well prepared for this encounter. If she does want to change her usual routine, this must be planned in advance, and she must be ready to interact with the class immediately when they arrive. From the word go, when she flaps at them to leave her room, she is sowing the seeds for a negative lesson. In fact, her very first word is 'No'! When they start to come into the room (as they are used to doing) she acts as though they are trespassing on her space. This inconsistency is bound to set up at least minor confrontations.

Her next mistake is to pick on poor James – a well-behaved student who is simply doing what he normally does, getting ready for the lesson! She immediately asks him what is 'wrong with him', and she compounds this rudeness when she tells him to 'shut up'. From the minute the teacher waved the students outside, there was a feeling of disquiet about this lesson: it is not surprising that they do not follow her instructions. Again, she is rude to them. She then picks on James unfairly (he is trying to get one of the other students to be quiet) and gives him an unearned sanction. If James was a confrontational student, this could have led to a more serious incident.

The class are now confused and bored – they had arrived at the lesson expecting consistency, and things are not turning out as normal. Because they are not fulfilling her (unrealistic) expectations, the teacher loses her temper. This does quieten the class down, but she then allows the students inside without having their full attention. At this stage, it seems to have been totally pointless for her to insist that they go outside and line up – she has achieved nothing! The 'troublemakers' at the back of the line have got away with their misbehaviour, and the lining-up activity is therefore pretty meaningless. At this point, it is likely that the class will take a long time to settle once inside the room, and they will have a negative view of the whole encounter.

Chewing gum

Age group: 13–15 years

Details: chewing gum is not allowed in the school. A few disruptive members of the class are consistently ignoring this rule, and using it as a way to try to establish that they can do what they want. The head has asked teachers to crack down on this minor rule-breaking.

A good example
The class are working on an individual task. Mr Everall is going around the room, helping them. He notices that Sundip is chewing. He goes to the front of the classroom, picks up the bin, and holds it out for Sundip.

Mr Everall: Sundip! Gum in the bin. Now. You know the rule.
Sundip: But, Sir! I'm not chewing.
Mr Everall: Yes you are. Spit it out. NOW.
Sundip: I've swallowed it, Sir. Look. [*He opens his mouth wide.*]
Mr Everall: I'll take your word on that, Sundip. But if I catch you chewing again this lesson, you're in big trouble.

Later on in the lesson, Mr Everall notices that Sundip is chewing again.

Mr Everall: Sundip. I want you to come over here, thanks. [*He walks over to the bin.*]

Sundip: What, Sir?

Mr Everall: Over here, thanks.

Sundip comes over to where the teacher is standing.

Mr Everall: See that?

Sundip: What?

Mr Everall: The bin.

Sundip: What about it?

Mr Everall leans towards Sundip and speaks quietly in his ear so that none of the class can hear.

Mr Everall: Put the gum in there NOW. And don't give me 'I'm not chewing', because I saw you. You can stay behind for 5 minutes after the lesson to clean up my room. Any more rubbish from you, and you'll be in detention.

Sundip spits out the gum and sheepishly goes to sit back down.

Commentary on the good example

These older students require a slightly different, no-nonsense approach. Because there is a disruptive element in the group, it is essential that the teacher makes his control of the situation very clear. His first approach is to demand in front of the whole class that the student puts the gum in the bin: the class already knows the rule about no gum and this student is plainly disobeying. Although this might seem quite a minor problem, if the teacher clamps down on it now, his overall authority will be reinforced because he has shown himself willing to apply all the school rules.

As often happens, the student claims to have already swallowed the gum, thus making the teacher's demand void. Instead of getting into a big scene about this, the teacher warns the student of what will happen if he is caught again. Later on in the lesson, the same situation arises. This time, the teacher takes a different approach, dealing with it in a more private way. He gets the student to come to him (a useful way of showing your high status) and then demands that he put the gum into the bin, making it perfectly clear that this time, the student must not 'try it on'. He then sanctions the student as promised, making the punishment fit the crime and warning him that any further disobedience will result in a worse penalty.

A bad example

The class are working on an individual task. Mr Everall is going around the room, helping them. He notices that Sundip is chewing.

Mr Everall:	Sundip? Are you chewing?
Sundip:	No, Sir.
Mr Everall:	Yes you are. I saw you.
Sundip:	No I'm not, Sir. Look. [*He opens his mouth wide.*]
Mr Everall:	I saw you chewing. Don't give me that rubbish. Could you go and spit the gum in the bin please?
Sundip:	But, Sir. I'm not chewing.
Mr Everall:	You'd better not be.

Later on in the lesson, Mr Everall notices that Sundip is chewing again.

Mr Everall:	Sundip. I thought you said you weren't chewing?
Sundip:	I'm not. I'm just biting the inside of my mouth. I do that when I'm bored.
Mr Everall:	Are you sure?
Sundip:	Absolutely sure.
Mr Everall:	Okay then.

Commentary on the bad example

This example is 'bad', not because a confrontation occurs, but because the student ends up getting one over on the teacher. In a class where there are troublemakers, this can be a dangerous precedent, because if a student gets away with minor misbehaviour like this, he starts to push the boundaries to see exactly how far he can go before being sanctioned. It is your decision as a teacher whether or not you apply rules such as the banning of chewing gum with these older students. You need to ask yourself: is it worth the confrontations that might occur? And can you use the rule to demonstrate your control over the class in a calm and consistent way?

The teacher's style here is very defensive. He asks the student whether he is chewing, rather than stating that he has seen him doing so. He also avoids sanctioning the student, perhaps because he is nervous about what might happen if he does. In this example, the student clearly wins the encounter – all the 'certain' statements are made by the student, rather than by the teacher. The comment that Sundip makes about being 'bored' hints at the contempt he feels towards the teacher and the lesson.

The threat of physical aggression

Age group: 16+ years

Details: Colin is a very difficult student, whose temper flares easily and often. During a lesson, he becomes involved in an argument with Patrick that quickly threatens to turn into a physical fight.

A good example
Colin and Patrick are arguing about who owns a DVD. Colin claims that he lent it to Patrick, but Patrick disagrees.

Colin:	Give it back, you ******!
Patrick:	Forget it, Colin. It's mine. You never lent it to me.
Miss Cook:	Colin. Patrick. I need you both to calm down please.
Colin:	He nicked my DVD, Miss.
Patrick:	He called me a ******, Miss!
Miss Cook:	Look, I want you both to get on with your work. And I want you to stop using foul language straight away, before I stop pretending not to hear you. Otherwise you'll force me to use the disciplinary policy and punish you for it. Give me the DVD, Patrick, and we'll sort this out at the end of the lesson.
Patrick:	No way. It's my DVD.

| Miss Cook: | Patrick. Give me the DVD **NOW**. No arguing. Be grown up about this. And go and sit over there away from Colin. [*She points to the far side of the classroom.*] |

He hands it over grudgingly and moves to sit across the room. The boys settle to work, but a few minutes later they start arguing again across the classroom.

Colin:	I'm gonna get you at break, you ****.
Patrick:	Oh yeah? Well I'm gonna mash your head you stupid ******!
Miss Cook:	Right, that's enough. Colin, Patrick. Outside NOW.
Patrick:	I'm not going outside. I ain't done nothin'.
Miss Cook:	Both of you outside NOW. I mean it. Don't mess with me.

The boys and Miss Cook go outside the room. She stands between them so that they can't get to each other.

Miss Cook:	Right. We're going to sort this out now. I have the DVD, and if there's any more rubbish about fighting from either of you, I'm going to give it to the principal. Then he can decide whether or not you get it back. Patrick? What do you say? Are you going to get on with your work? No more nonsense?
Patrick:	All right, Miss.
Miss Cook:	Good. Very sensible. Right. You go inside. I want to talk to Colin on his own. [*Patrick goes back in.*]
Colin:	I'm gonna punch him, Miss. I don't care what you say.
Miss Cook:	Colin. You are making me extremely unhappy with this attitude. If you punch Patrick, you'll get yourself into trouble. You'll probably get thrown out for good. Is that what you really want?
Colin:	No.
Miss Cook:	I want us to sort this out by talking about it. Tell me about the DVD.
Colin:	My sister bought it for me. I lent it to Patrick, but he won't give it back. He's a ****.

Miss Cook:	Colin, I'm going to pretend I didn't hear that, because if I did hear it I would feel very offended. But if you push it again I am going to have to give you a disciplinary slip.
Colin:	Sorry, Miss.
Miss Cook:	Right. Could we find your sister at break time and check with her? If she agrees with what you say, then you can have the DVD back.
Colin:	Okay.
Miss Cook:	Right, Colin. Now I want you to sit out here to work for the rest of the lesson.
Colin:	Why? That's not fair.
Miss Cook:	Do you want to get into a fight with Patrick? No? Well, I'm saving you the temptation if you sit outside. We'll sort out your DVD at break, Okay?

Colin agrees. Miss Cook brings him out a desk and chair to work at, leaving her door open so she can keep an eye on him.

Commentary on the good example

The teacher intervenes quickly as the argument starts, hoping to stop it before it develops. Such early intervention can often prevent a minor confrontation spiralling out of control. She chooses to ignore the bad language that Colin has used, because she knows that this will only exacerbate this particular situation. These are older students, and for many of them swearing is the normal way of communicating anger – she feels that there is no point in making a big deal out of it. She needs to get the DVD off the students quickly, because that will solve the problem temporarily: if she has the DVD then she can decide what is done with it. If Patrick keeps the DVD, it is likely that Colin will try to get it off him physically. Her tone is very clear and direct – she tells him to give it to her NOW, rather than asking him. She also separates the two boys, hoping that this will stop the argument immediately.

Unfortunately, the conflict resumes a few minutes later, and the teacher realizes that she must take further action to settle it. The boys swear at each other, and threaten physical violence. This is unacceptable, and the teacher removes them from the room to talk to them further. By doing this, she can deal with the problem away from the rest of the class. The class can get on with their work rather than watching her talk to the boys. Again, the teacher tells them very firmly that they must go outside – she will take no argument on this point.

Once outside, the teacher uses the DVD as a bargaining tool while talking to the boys – if they do keep arguing she will pass it to the principal. She hopes that this threat will calm them down. She deals with Patrick first – he is the less aggressive of the two and she has no real wish to punish him. After sending him back inside, she can deal with Colin in a more peaceful atmosphere. Unfortunately, Colin continues with his aggressive stance. The teacher is well aware of how easily Colin can be 'set off', and she maintains a very calm but firm manner with him. She points out to him what will happen if he does go ahead and hit Patrick. Then she allows Colin to tell his side of the story – by listening to him and taking his points seriously, she shows her human side and she also shows that she is willing to believe and trust him.

Colin swears again, and again the teacher chooses to ignore it, but this time she issues a final warning, and makes it clear that she finds his language offensive. She then offers a solution, one that is deferred to break time, when she will have a better chance to deal with the problem. She is aware that she needs to get back inside to her class now. Finally, she asks Colin to sit outside for the rest of the lesson, thus avoiding the possibility of further physical confrontation. Notice how firm the teacher's tone has been in dealing with this whole situation, while at the same time remaining calm and non-confrontational. She tells them what to do, rather than asking them, thus maintaining a feeling that she is in control, no matter how nervous she feels inside. Notice too how she uses their names repeatedly, ensuring that she has their full attention when she is talking to them.

A bad example
Colin and Patrick are arguing about who owns a DVD. Colin claims that he lent it to Patrick, but Patrick disagrees.

Colin: Give it back, you ******!

Patrick:	Get real, Colin. It's mine. You never lent it to me.
Miss Cook:	Boys. Will you please stop arguing?
Colin:	He nicked my DVD, Miss.
Patrick:	He called me a ******, Miss!
Miss Cook:	[*sounding very irritated*] Look, will you both stop using such foul language and get on with your work now. Do you want to be in detention with me after the lesson? No? Well, would you shut up then and get back to work.

The boys grudgingly settle to work, but a few minutes later they start arguing again.

Colin:	I'm gonna get you later, you ****.
Patrick:	Oh yeah? Well I'm gonna mash your head right now you stupid ******!

The boys are on their feet, taking up threatening postures.

Miss Cook:	Right. Stop that now. Sit down.
Colin:	You ain't gonna mash my head, you thick *******!
Patrick:	Oh yeah? Come on then, Colin. You think you're hard. [*He holds up his fists.*]
Miss Cook:	WILL YOU STOP IT AND SIT DOWN!!

It is too late, the boys are already fighting, and the rest of the class is urging them on. Miss Cook tries to get to them to separate them.

The Class:	Fight! Fight! Fight! Fight!
Miss Cook:	WILL YOU ALL STOP IT AND SIT DOWN NOW!!

Commentary on the bad example

Notice how quickly the fight escalates here, because the teacher does not intervene firmly enough right at the beginning. Instead of telling the students what she wants, she asks them to stop arguing. She also calls them 'boys', instead of addressing them by name, which lessens the impact of what she says. She threatens a detention as a way of solving the problem, rather than moving into the quarrel and removing the cause of friction, the DVD. She also asks them to 'shut up', rather than telling them to 'be quiet'. By reflecting their own attitude in this way, and using an irritated tone, she is more likely to add to the conflict than to dissipate it.

After a few minutes the conflict is still there, and the boys start arguing again. Because the teacher did not intervene sufficiently early, it is now too late for her to stop a physical quarrel taking place. Again, she tells them to sit down rather than moving in to separate them or to take them outside, away from the class. But it is all too late – the fight is inevitable.

PART FOUR

When Things get Tough

14

Managing confrontation

Why do confrontations arise?

There is a range of complex reasons why confrontations arise. Sometimes the cause will be entirely outside of your control – a student arrives at your classroom in such a tense and worked-up state that there is little you can do beyond containing the situation. Some students carry with them a huge weight of metaphorical baggage – horrible situations and events experienced outside of the school setting that make them far more likely to blow a fuse. Some will have learnt by example, from parents or guardians who react to problems in a confrontational manner. Wherever possible, within the bounds of confidentiality, it is worth your having at least some idea of the kind of home lives that your students lead. You can then be sensitive to their particular circumstances, applying the flexibility discussed at the start of this book.

At other times, though, the teacher makes a direct contribution to the confrontation. While it is not the teacher's *fault* that the student loses control, he does certain things to exacerbate the situation. In your quest to manage behaviour better, it is important to understand how you might contribute to confrontations, so that you can avoid them whenever possible. Here are some ways that the teacher can help create the climate for a confrontation. (Please note, these are all mistakes I have made myself!)

- **The mood of the teacher:** when you begin a lesson in a bad mood, this attitude filters through and puts everyone in the room in a negative frame of mind. You might be unnecessarily picky or uncompromising with the students, and generate an atmosphere of tension and anger.

- **A sense of unfairness**: students are very sensitive to actual or perceived unfairness. We would all hope to be completely fair all or most of the time. However, we need to be aware how our personal feelings about individuals can subconsciously come out in the way that we treat them.

- **Misunderstandings**: sometimes the teacher accuses a student or class of misbehaviour and is entirely wrong. I once caught some students passing around what I assumed was a note at the back of the room. When I insisted they hand it over, they refused and I got cross. In the end it turned out that they were all signing a thank-you card for me. Whoops.

- **Playing to the 'audience'**: if you take on a rude student in front of the class, this sets the stage for a confrontation. While some students will back down, others will be unable or unwilling to do so, and will get themselves trapped into a slanging match with you.

- **Lack of consistency**: where the teacher is inconsistent, this can create a sense of injustice and consequently lead to tensions. It might be that the teacher applies the rules differently from other staff in the school. It could be that the teacher varies his expectations from day to day. The more consistent you are, the more your students will know what to expect from you.

- **Prejudging the student or class**: once a student gets a reputation, it can be hard to shift. Similarly, a class is sometimes known as 'difficult' by a number of staff. When the teacher meets a student or a class with preset expectations, it means the students are never given the chance to prove themselves. Again, this can create a sense of injustice and consequently lead to tension and confrontation.

How to avoid confrontation

Wherever possible, it is obviously far preferable to avoid getting into confrontations in the first place: they can only ever do damage to the relationship between you and your students. In addition, there is always the risk that a negative encounter might spiral out of control into physical aggression.

Problems can occur particularly when the teacher is tired and stressed. A student swears at you or behaves in a completely inappropriate way, and it is all too easy (and natural) to want to confront the behaviour in a similarly hostile way, thus escalating the situation. Avoiding confrontation does not mean you avoid dealing with the issue, but rather that you approach the problem in a sensitive manner. When handling a confrontational student, try using the following techniques:

- ✓ **Be an assertive, confident and consistent teacher**: if you manage the class in an effective and assertive way all or most of the time, you should be rewarded with lower levels of tension within the group.
- ✓ **Be aware of your emotional state**: on those days when you are tired or tense, have an awareness of how this might affect your classroom management skills. Minimize potential stress by keeping lesson activities simple and controlled. Make sure you take your breaks and leave school on time to get a good rest.
- ✓ **Keep difficult interactions private**: learn to talk with and sanction students in a private way, so that there is no risk of them playing up to the audience.
- ✓ **Make an early intervention**: keep an eye out for the early signs of any problems. If you notice an argument starting, or a student becoming restless, intervene straight away.
- ✓ **Know when to ignore low-level misbehaviour**: on the other hand, know when it is appropriate to simply ignore silliness, rather than making an issue out of attention-seeking behaviour.
- ✓ **Refuse to enter into tit-for-tat arguments**: some students love to drag the teacher into an argument: it means they don't have to work; they might even be able to deflect the blame for misbehaviour. Don't get pulled in – it is pointless and can lead to unnecessary tension. Remember – 'be reasonable but don't reason with them'.
- ✓ **Change the subject**: try using a distraction to dissipate a potential confrontation. Just as, when a baby is crying, you might try pulling a silly face or shaking a favourite toy, so by changing

the subject with your students, you could throw them 'off the track' of their aggression.

✓ **Defer the issue:** there will be occasions when you are involved in an interaction and it becomes clear that the student is simply not going to do as you ask, and instead is getting increasingly agitated or aggressive. In these cases, it can help to defer the whole discussion until a later time, for instance saying 'we'll discuss this at the end of class'.

✓ **Be willing to apologize when you get it wrong:** when you do make a mistake, for instance if you're rude or unnecessarily aggressive with a student or the class, have the humility to apologize. This will earn you a great deal of respect.

How to deal with confrontation

Once a confrontation gets started, some students find it incredibly difficult to back down. As the adult, and the professional person, it is your responsibility to try to deal with the situation in the best way possible. The ideal is for you to manage the situation so that the least damage is done to the relationship between you and your students, while at the same time ensuring the safety of everyone in your class. The following suggestions should help you achieve this.

Behaviour management techniques:

✓ **'Remove' the problem:** often, confrontation is about a 'thing', whether this is a pencil case, a CD, a mobile phone, and so on. If possible, get the 'thing' out of the equation. Take care with using confiscation as your first approach – this can escalate tensions. Instead, insist that the student puts the item away in a bag before you are forced to take it away. Sometimes you might 'remove' the student, asking him to step outside the room for a moment, to calm himself down. Make sure the student is not left alone: ask a teaching assistant to go with him or leave the door open.

✓ **Take feelings and complaints seriously:** sometimes it is enough simply to listen. Ask the student to describe the problem that has led to the blow-up and make the right sympathetic noises.

✓ **Know when to send for help**: there is no shame at all in sending a reliable student to get a senior manager if a fight breaks out in your room, or if a situation escalates beyond where you feel comfortable. This will help you handle the situation, and also provide you with a witness to what takes place.

✓ **Remain calm**: it's very difficult for a student to sustain feelings of anger if he has nothing to feed off. Stay calm and it's hard for your students to maintain a confrontational manner. It also demonstrates a powerful positive role model of how to handle aggression.

✓ **Pause for a moment**: when a situation erupts, the temptation is to jump straight in to sort it out. Take a few seconds to think first – giving yourself time to calm down can help you handle a tricky situation in the best possible way.

The teacher's use of voice/body:

✓ **Use a hypnotic tone of voice**: your voice can be very helpful in calming tense situations. Use a slow monotone to dampen down heightened emotions.

✓ **Use low-key body language**: similarly, non-confrontational postures and body language can help calm things down. Make sure you keep out of the student's personal space – not only to lessen the tension, but also to protect yourself from physical attack.

✓ **Make repeated use of names**: repeating a student's name will help you get his attention and might even allow you to pull him back from the confrontation. Combine this with a low-key and hypnotic tone of voice.

✓ **Remember, it's not about win or lose**: teachers can get trapped into feeling that they have to 'win' a confrontation. The reality is that nobody really wins, no matter what happens in the end. Your aim should be to calm things down, not to end up feeling that you won.

✓ **You don't have to make eye contact**: we are so used to having eye contact with our students and our classes that it is tempting to get locked into a 'look at me when I'm talking to you' attitude. Sometimes, a better approach is to talk to the student without looking him directly in the eye. This applies particularly to those from cultural backgrounds where direct eye contact is seen as rude or threatening.

Handling the aftermath

When a confrontation takes place in one of your lessons, you may find yourself feeling shaky and upset. You might also suffer a dip in self-confidence and feel that you have somehow 'failed' as a teacher. A good school or college will understand that serious confrontations can have a severe impact on staff, and there will be support available to help you manage your emotions. The following suggestions should hopefully help you to cope and to bounce back quickly.

- ✓ Give yourself some time to recover – if possible, ask for your next lesson to be covered so that you get a chance to rest.
- ✓ Record what happened: get hold of an incident form and write about the confrontation while the details are fresh in your mind. Note the names of witnesses where appropriate.
- ✓ Find support wherever it is available, whether this is from managers, a union, other teachers, or perhaps outside of the school environment.
- ✓ Try not to take the situation personally – a student who is verbally or physically abusive obviously has some serious problems.
- ✓ Try not to bear grudges – aim to give the student a 'fresh start' the next time you have to teach him.

Teaching in the toughest settings

Some of the people reading this book will be teaching in a really difficult school or college. Although any teaching job is going to be a challenge, some settings are at the far end of the scale of 'toughness'. Typically, in the 'toughest' settings:

- The overall ethos of the setting has become negative and hopeless.
- The students don't feel that their teachers or the managers can control them.
- There is a high turnover of staff.
- Because staff leave so quickly, there is no time to build up relationships.
- Students feel that staff 'don't care' because they keep leaving.
- They are more likely to 'act up' for new teachers to test them out and see whether they can cope.
- The students start to 'believe their own publicity', and begin to feel that they have to live up to their reputation.
- The setting has a bad reputation locally, and this leads to a fall in student numbers. Only those who 'have to' go there do.
- There are larger than usual numbers of students with learning difficulties or severe behavioural issues.

Some teachers work in a 'tough' environment for many years: they stick it out and become part of the backbone of the setting. Other teachers find the pressure hard to handle, or simply do not want to work in this kind of place.

If you're working in a really tough setting:

✓ **Put yourself first**: practise the art of 'selfish altruism'. The idea is that, by being selfish and looking after yourself as a priority, you put yourself in a much better position to help your students. It also means that you are more likely to survive in a really tough setting in the long run. This means you must take your breaks – be firm with yourself about spending time away from the students. Give yourself permission to teach a less-than-perfect lesson when you're not on top form, without feeling guilty about it.
✓ **Work out your priorities**: set yourself some simple, key priorities and stick to these. Work out what you can realistically ask for and get in terms of behaviour, without pulling yourself into endless confrontations. Focus on getting learning to happen, rather than on getting everything exactly as you wish before

you start the lesson. That is not to say that you should lower your standards; rather, that you must work out what your 'non-negotiables' are, and stick to them as far as you humanly can.

✓ **Understand student reputations**: in a tough school, the students will quickly learn how important it is to build themselves a 'reputation'. Those who are strongest, who have the quickest wits, or who are willing to challenge authority, will gain a status that puts them near the top of the peer group heap. Behaviour issues in your classroom might often involve a student trying to assert his reputation. If you can get these 'high status' individuals on your side, you have much more chance of winning over the rest of the group.

✓ **Don't pass the buck**: in a tough school, metaphorical 'fires' are breaking out all the time, and all over the place. What I mean is, there will be incidents going on in each classroom, and probably in the corridors as well. In a tough school, you have to deal with your own situations where humanly possible, rather than calling for a more senior teacher. This increases your reputation for effectiveness, and allows senior staff to focus on keeping overall control.

A very helpful, honest book for those in the toughest teaching situations is Paul Blum's *Surviving and Succeeding in Difficult Classrooms* (2006, London: Routledge).

15

Managing stress

I can't cope anymore!

There's no doubt that teaching is a difficult profession in which to work. It is emotionally, physically and psychologically taxing, and there may be times when you do feel as though you just can't cope anymore. No matter how hard you try, you feel that you are making no headway in improving the behaviour of your students. This is extremely demoralizing. Day after day, you arrive at your job, only to face students who simply will not behave. You begin to dread coming into work, knowing that you have to face such a difficult day.

At these times, it is important to differentiate between the inevitable ups and downs of a teaching career, and the signs of a more serious problem. Once you've identified exactly what the problem is, you can explore some suitable options for dealing with it.

What's the problem?

The feeling that you can't cope anymore can build up slowly, or it can arrive without warning one day, when you feel that you simply can't get out of bed and go into work. Sometimes, the problem is a temporary one, and one that can be dealt with relatively easily. On the other hand, it could be a more long-term issue, and one that will require more extreme measures to solve. Here are some thoughts about what the problem might be.

Seasonal effects

The time of the year can have a huge impact on your ability to cope with difficult behaviour. In September you will be fresh and full of energy, ready to deal with whatever the students can throw at you. Of course, this is the time when you most need this extra energy. It is extremely stressful to be meeting new people, learning new names, and, if you are new at your school or setting, finding your way around the building, the systems, and so on.

Towards the end of the first term, energy levels fall low, the nights become darker and the students more fractious. Ask yourself – is the feeling that I can't cope a symptom of general tiredness? Will things seem better at the beginning of a new term, when I've had a holiday and I feel refreshed and ready to face my students again? If this is the case, try to have a proper break from teaching during your holidays. Refuse to take any planning or marking home with you, book yourself a flight to somewhere sunny, and concentrate on recharging your batteries. That way you can plunge in with renewed vigour when you return to school next term.

Overwork

It could be that you are tired because you are overworked. If you take on too much outside of lesson time, this can lead to problems dealing with your classroom teaching. You may have family or other commitments that cause you additional stress and leave you too exhausted to deal properly with managing the behaviour of your students.

Think very carefully about your extra-curricular responsibilities. Although these activities offer a welcome change from classroom teaching, and a good opportunity to get to know your students, they also mean that you have to stay late after a full working day. Your number-one priority has to be your health and sanity – learn to say 'no' to demands on your time when your stress levels are too high. The term 'selfish altruism' applies here – be selfish enough to take care of yourself, so you're in the best possible state to help your students learn.

The setting

On the other hand, it could be the school or college itself that is the problem: remember, your working environment has a powerful impact on behaviour in your classroom. Are your school buildings run-down and uncared for? Is the ethos a negative and confrontational one? Is there poor continuity of staff and a management that does not support you properly? And is the behaviour policy ineffective in dealing with the issues that you face? If you have answered 'yes' to some or all of these questions, then it is likely that your setting is struggling with difficult behaviour.

If this is your situation, make sure you turn to other staff for support. And if you feel that your personal situation is getting out of hand, and that you alone cannot even start to improve the situation at your school or college, then you will need to decide whether you are willing to stay. The most important thing is for you personally to stay healthy and happy – you won't be an effective teacher if you are unhappy or ill.

Your personality

Different people react differently to different situations. Some teachers seem able to shrug off incidents of misbehaviour, putting any problems behind them and moving quickly onwards. Other teachers take the same kind of incidents to heart, and find it almost impossible to wipe them from memory. Many of us do get very emotionally involved with the job – it's almost inevitable when you are working with young people, some of whom lead very troubled lives. But if you are a sensitive person, you will need to learn to cope with your emotional responses, particularly if you teach in a challenging school.

What are the danger signs?

A certain amount and type of stress is healthy: it is essential in keeping us energetic and 'alive', and keeps us from becoming dissatisfied with our work. After all, you probably came into teaching because you would have been bored by a typical office job. Teaching offers many different challenges, and it can be the most wonderful career in the world. On the other hand, a difficult teaching job can be too much for some people to manage, and there is no shame at all attached to feeling that you cannot cope.

Stress is a response to a difficult situation, and when we are stressed we produce high levels of adrenaline. Originally, the production of adrenaline helped us in a fight-or-flight situation, where our ancestors needed to be ready to flee from danger or to wrestle the proverbial mammoth to the ground. The problem in our modern world is that we have become overstressed, producing all this adrenaline without any means of using it up.

As a teacher, you have to stay and deal with stressful cir-cumstances, rather than running away or resorting to physical solutions. If your school situation is problematic, and your stress levels are too high, your health could be put at risk, and not even the most wonderful career in the world is worth that. The symp-toms of stress vary according to the individual, but there are some common signs that you could look out for to check whether you are becoming excessively stressed by your work.

Physical symptoms

- **Difficulty sleeping**: if you are having difficulty sleeping, particularly on a Sunday night when you are preparing for the week ahead, you could well be experiencing high levels of work-related stress. Do you dream about your problem classes? And do your dreams become nightmares in which you can no longer cope?
- **Feeling sick**: that hollow feeling in the pit of the stomach is, I'm sure, something that many teachers, and certainly all those who have worked in a school where there are serious behaviour issues, can relate to. Do you feel sick when you are about to face your most difficult class, or classes? Or do you have that sick feeling all the time? If you do, it is likely that you are suffering from excessive stress.
- **Increased heart rate**: you might also find that your heart begins to beat faster because of the production of adrenaline. Does this happen to you when you are about to teach? Again, a raised heart rate can be a symptom of stress.

- **Sweaty palms:** if your palms become sweaty in tense classroom situations, this could be a further sign that you are over-stressed.

Emotional symptoms

- **Loss of confidence:** when you feel that you can't cope with the behaviour of your students, it is easy to lose confidence in your teaching abilities. Your perception of what is actually happening in your classroom can become distorted, and the problems you are experiencing might loom much larger than they are in reality.
- **Becoming defensive:** you might also find that you become overly defensive, expecting the worst from your students. This can be very counterproductive and can lead to a negative attitude towards your work and your students.
- **Bursting into tears:** all too often, I have seen teachers (including myself) reduced to tears in the staffroom, or even in the classroom. What other job forces this sort of humiliation on its workers? If you find yourself feeling overly vulnerable and emotional, this is probably a sign of very high stress levels.
- **Becoming snappy:** when you or your colleagues are stressed, the temptation to snap at each other becomes greater, particularly if you are all dealing with similarly difficult students. Again, poor relationships among the staff in a school can indicate a time of high stress, perhaps during an inspection or other stressful event.

How do you cope?

How, then, do you cope if your stress levels are high, and you feel that behaviour management problems are getting on top of you? First, follow the advice given in this book. Many of the tips that I give are simple to put in place, but will make a huge difference to behaviour in your classes. The strategies could take a while to work, so don't lose heart if they don't make an immediate difference. With persistence, you will start to make inroads into your problems. In the meantime, here are a few specific ideas for managing high stress levels.

Use your support systems

In my experience, the staff who work in schools are wonderful at supporting their colleagues. Use all the support systems that are available to you: an induction tutor, a SENCO, a fellow teacher, a teaching assistant, plus friends and family too. Talk about your problems with someone sympathetic – sometimes all that is needed is a shoulder to cry on, or a caring ear in which to pour out your woes.

It can be very helpful to watch another teacher's classes, someone who you know has excellent classroom control. Although this option is usually only offered to newly qualified teachers, a supportive head might allow you to do some observations if you explain how helpful the opportunity would be. By watching how someone else copes with similar students to your own, you will pick up some useful tips that you can utilize in your own classroom.

If you watch a teacher who has been at the school for a while, don't forget the power of a good reputation. If you are new to the school, you will still be building up your own positive word of mouth. Similarly, if you watch a member of staff who has a management post (head of department, head of year, deputy head), remember that this responsibility will also have an impact on how the students behave.

Keep a perspective

In a difficult school it is sometimes hard to keep a perspective on what you are really achieving. At primary level, you will be wholly or mainly responsible for teaching one class – no one else is having to cope with exactly this mix of children. At secondary and college level, a major problem is that you never get to see the students in their other classes, and so you have no real idea of how they behave for their other teachers. Always remember, a badly behaved class is not necessarily a reflection of your talents as a teacher, but is a manifestation of many other contributing factors. Remember, too, that at the end of the day the world really is not going to end if your students won't behave themselves. Try to avoid blowing up incidents of poor behaviour into more than they really are. Bear this great quote in mind: 'Even in your worst lesson, nobody died.'

React from the head

Our instinctive reaction to rudeness or aggression is to take it to heart – we are human beings and not machines, after all. But every time teachers become emotional, this causes them stress and also shows the students that they can 'win' by misbehaving. Some students love 'winding up' their teachers, and when we react emotionally, they have succeeded. On the other hand, maintaining a rational, intellectual response will show the students that they cannot get at you. It will also help you think of ways to manage the situation in a calm and considered way.

Every time you feel your heart starting to race, and your emotions kicking in, take a moment to think about the situation from your head, rather than from your heart. Pause for a few seconds, to cut the link between your emotional response and your actual reaction. Respond in a logical, thinking way, rather than in a sensitive, feeling way. Here are a couple of examples to illustrate the point:

The disruptive student

Meredith is wandering around the room, disturbing the rest of the class and refusing to sit back down, despite being warned about possible sanctions.

Your heart says: *'Why won't she do what I say? The rest of the class must think I've got no control over her. I feel so helpless. Now I'm getting angry. WHY WON'T YOU DO WHAT I SAY, MEREDITH?!'*

Your head says: *'Okay, this student is refusing to do what I say, but it's not my fault, it's her own choice. Now, what am I going to do about it? Well, first of all I'll stay calm, that's important. Then I'll warn her, and if that doesn't work, impose the sanctions that I've told the class about.'*

The uncontrollable class

Your class is an extremely difficult one, and they are totally refusing to settle down and get on with their work. They are making loads of noise and throwing paper aeroplanes around the room.

Your heart says: *'Help!!! They're completely out of control! What am I going to do!? Someone might hear them and think that I can't control my classes. I'm never ever going to be able to get them settled down and teach them! Why on earth did I decide to become a teacher?'*

Your head says: *'Okay, things are going wrong here, but I'm not going to panic. First of all, it's not my fault, it's the students who have decided to misbehave. And everyone says what a difficult class this is. I'll try and apply the sanctions I've set, and if necessary I'll have to keep the whole class in. I know, I'll write "whole-class detention?" on the board and see if that helps.'*

Take heart from small successes

When you are feeling really down, consider the small steps your students have taken that might make you feel proud. For a teacher in a difficult school, or working with a difficult class, getting your students to stay in their chairs may represent a huge achievement. Praise and reward yourself, as well as your students, for these achievements. Teaching is a complex job, and there are many people who could not even start to make the progress you have made. Take a look at what your good students are achieving as well: often, when we are dealing with generally poor behaviour, it becomes easy to overlook the work and attitudes of our well-behaved students.

'The caring stops at five o'clock'

This line (given to me by a teacher who worked in a pupil referral unit) perfectly sums up the need to be able to cut off from the job, especially if you are a sensitive soul. It is inevitable that, to an extent, you will take the job home with you. But if you wish to stay in the profession for the long term, you must accept that you cannot change the world. You will probably come across children, teenagers, young people and adults whose lives outside of school are pretty miserable, but your main role is as a teacher and not as a social worker. Do the best that you can during working hours, but leave school behind when you head home for the day.

Don't be a perfectionist

You simply can't be a perfectionist if you're a teacher – the job is far too complex and multifaceted to get it right all the time. When a lesson goes wrong, look for reasons by all means, but don't bog yourself down with excessive self-analysis. If a student chooses to opt out of your subject, try your best, but don't beat yourself up about it. As long as you are doing the best that you can for your students, then you are doing your job. There is no point in dwelling on what is past and gone – keep learning, but always look to the future.

Take time out

There is no shame in sometimes making life easy for yourself, particularly if you are dealing with difficult students on a daily basis. On occasions, give yourself a break, perhaps by showing a DVD, or going to the computer room.

Take time off

If you are suffering from high stress levels, go to visit your doctor. It could be that you are ill, and that you need to take some time off to recover. Similarly, when you have the flu, see that as a signal to have some time off sick, rather than muddling through until you can't go on anymore. Do not feel embarrassed or ashamed if you need to take sick leave. Teaching is an extremely taxing profession, and you will not be able to work at your best if you are tense and stressed. Above all, make your own health your first priority.

Get out!?

At some stage, you might have to ask yourself whether you are willing to cope anymore with your school, or with teaching as a profession. This is a personal choice that only you can make, but one that you will obviously want to consider long and hard. It could be that you have become disillusioned with your current school, but that changing to a job somewhere else will refresh your outlook on teaching as a career. Only you can decide.

Whether you do decide to change jobs, or to change careers, I wish you all the best in your future. And please don't forget, teachers make a huge difference to the lives of all their students. There are so many well-behaved ones out there who need your talents and your help. And your poorly behaved students are in desperate need of your care and attention to help them succeed, no matter how much they might push you away. So, follow the advice in this book, keep plugging away, and I promise you that you will be successful in 'getting the buggers to behave'!

SWINDON COLLEGE

LEARNING RESOURCE CENTRE

Index

music 17, 51, 74, 87, 90, 144,
160, 189
mystique 82

names of students 25, 34–6, 154,
174, 194, 239
needs of students 19, 24–5, 121,
135–6, 138, 166, 174 *see also*
special educational needs
noise 21, 102–3, 152, 155–6,
185–6

outdoor lessons 152–3
overreactions 8, 53, 74–5, 122,
215
overwork 80, 244

pacing of lessons 26, 50–1, 64–5,
106, 130
partnership with students 201
passive teaching 75
pastoral role of teachers 206
pause, use of 42, 62, 66, 181, 239,
249
PE *see* physical education
peer pressure 53, 86, 88, 90, 123,
135–6, 190
pen pals 190–1
perfectionism 37, 251
persistence 19–20, 247
personality 26–7, 42, 57, 61, 69,
73, 77–8, 110, 245
perspective 53, 167, 248–9
physical education (PE) 43, 78,
128, 155
plasticine, flicking of 215–18
plenaries 14, 33, 106
points systems 89
politeness 5, 10, 12, 26, 42, 58–9,
76–7, 97, 220
positive outlook 15–16, 23, 37,
45, 61, 83–4, 87–8, 90–1, 130,
141, 154–5, 159–61, 172–3
posture 26, 60, 68, 75, 175,
239

practical activity 109–10, 150–2
praise 9, 15–16, 33, 89, 124, 129,
132, 134, 136, 217, 250
primary school students 20, 34–5,
171–91
privileges 90, 188
students' loss of 93, 151, 201
prizes 51, 90, 188
psychological aspects of teaching
71–2
purpose, sense of 14, 16

questions *see* asking questions
quizzes 107, 202

raffles 90
'reading' a class 40–1
reasoning with students 47–9,
136, 211–12, 237
'red card' system 10, 94, 166
registration of students 206
repetition, deliberate 49–50, 97,
183
reputations
of individual students 25, 136,
236, 241–2
of individual teachers 36,
82–3, 102, 194, 197, 242,
248
resources 117–18, 146
respect 7, 9, 17, 26, 34, 42, 58,
60, 69, 197
responsibility taken by students
45, 47, 96, 177, 180
review time 111
rewards 9, 18–19, 85–91, 163,
188, 207
rhetorical questions 11, 48
role models, teachers as 26, 58–9,
87, 132, 189, 239
routines 14, 30, 124, 126, 139,
143, 172, 177–8, 222
rudeness 58–9, 97, 122, 136,
249
'rule of three' 183